2025

International Journal of Narrative Therapy and Community Work

NUMBER TWO

International Journal of Narrative Therapy and Community Work is a peer-reviewed journal for practitioners who wish to stay in touch with the latest ideas and developments in narrative practice.
It is published twice a year on the equinoxes.

Publisher: .... Dulwich Centre Foundation
Editor-in-chief: .... Shelja Sen
Senior editor: .... David Denborough
Editorial consultant: ..... Cheryl White
Managing editor: .... Claire Nettle
Designer: .... Elite Design Studio
Contact: .... ijntcw@dulwichcentre.com.au

We welcome submissions. Please see details at https://dulwichcentre.com.au/information-for-authors/

ISSN: 2981-8818
ISBN: 978-0-6458385-5-8

For journal information and to access audio, video and multimedia content,
scan this QR code with your mobile device.

Dulwich Centre Foundation

PO Box 7192
Halifax Street Post Office
Adelaide/Tarntanya
Kaurna Country
South Australia, 5000

The views expressed in this journal are not necessarily those of the publisher.

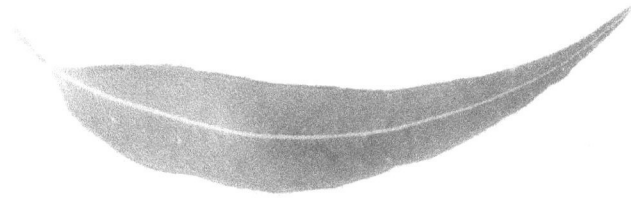

Editorial

Dear Reader

Too many people are up against horrifying injustices that are being perpetuated in an attempt to diminish their lives. Within these same contexts, there are stories of resistance, of people holding on to what is precious to them, of speaking up. Reminding us, yet again, that our work is situated in history, culture and politics. This edition is a testimony to the expansive possibilities of narrative practice and the ethics of solidarity.

Jack T. C. Chiu and Sharon S. K. Leung's human–canine project in Hong Kong considers what is absent but implicit in the social withdrawal of young people and their preference for animal connections. As they point out, "narrative practice offers a powerful framework for understanding youth withdrawal not as a personal failing but as a form of resistance" and a refusal to shape their identities and lives according to socially constructed norms.

Tracing another thread of resistance, Sandra Coral draws on critical race theory to bring attention to the Eurocentric leanings in therapy spaces, which often leave Black neurodivergent people unsafe. Sandra invites us to reflect on how "the more closely a person can generally adhere to and function under the expectations of the dominant culture, the more power they can usually access in society. But this behaviour alienates the colonised person from their communities". Narrative therapy and help us to create "pockets of freedom" – spaces free from the dominant culture's interpretations and judgements – as sites of refuge and resistance, responding to the alienation imposed by colonial legacies.

Stephanie Badman's work demonstrates this in the realm of genetic counselling, where the medicalised understandings often privilege professional knowledge over lived experience. Through letter writing, which elevates people's own local knowledges, narrative practice creates space for witnessing and re-witnessing preferred identities.

Christine Dennstedt takes us into the liminal encounters of psychedelic-assisted therapy and draws on the narrative practice metaphor of migration of identity to loosen entrenched problem stories and allow new meanings to take shape. She also examines our ethical accountability when engaging with practices linked to Indigenous knowledges, and the need for humility, integrity and a commitment to avoiding cultural appropriation.

Directing a narrative feminist lens on bulimia and abuse, Kassandra Pedersen proposes an alternative fluid language for bulimia, using the metaphor of tides. She offers a nuanced, justice-informed approach that avoids replicating neoliberal discourses on food and body management, in which the body is seen as a passive recipient of trauma. Instead, Kassandra invites us to respect the body's capacity to notice, disagree and bear witness.

In a deeply moving contribution, Tanya Newman shares the voices of dying mothers who write letters for their children. These letters are not only acts of love but also portals to future re-membering, enabling both mothers and children to resist single-storied descriptions of loss. Through "linking lives", mothers leave behind an archive of care, preferred identities, and their unfinished yet enduring work of raising children.

Tarang Kaur turns our attention to neurodivergent children, whose skills, values and acts of resistance are too often pathologised by deficit-based discourses and disregarded in the name of treatment. Through living documents, we are invited to witness children as keen collaborators and bearers of unique insider knowledge. What is dismissed as "problematic behaviour" can be seen as a child's creative response and skilful reclaiming of agency.

The two audio recordings in this issue show us how people quietly resist erasure, remember those who came before, and shape futures rooted in dignity and care.

The first one, by Chelsea Size, weaves together wisdom on living with loneliness from residents in aged care, exploring stories of healing that can live alongside stories of loss. Their small yet profound practices, like a resident sharing, "I like the patterns in the clouds and the way they bring me calmness", show how memory, nature and everyday rituals can become companions in times of sadness, uncertainty and grief.

The second audio recording is from the archives. Aunty Barbara Wingard's paper shows us how grief itself can be spoken of in culturally sustaining ways. For First Nations people, conversations with grief are not only about sorrow but about refusing to be silenced, honouring ancestors and cherishing histories. As Aunty Barbara reminds us: "We are remembering those who have died, we are honouring Indigenous spiritual ways, and we are finding ways of grieving that bring us together. We are telling our stories in ways that make us stronger."

Lorraine Grieves, in the video recording "We have always been here, We've been here before", shares the we Are Allies project and asks us to reflect on how we can repair, redress and stay in relationship amidst systems built on white supremacy, colonisation and the rising tide of fascism and hatred. History reminds us that gender diversity has always existed across the world. In the face of divisiveness, disinformation and attempts to silence, we can draw on collective wisdom and discernment to support a long game of resistance that is built on hope and liberatory practices.

We are keen to revitalise the journal's review section. Over the journal's history, we have published review essays that stretch the field of narrative practice by making new connections, presenting innovative ideas or offering provocations. We particularly value reviews that draw connections between books (and other cultural works) and practice, and reviews that make original contributions in their own right. For this issue, David Denborough responded to a request to write three book reviews from diverse cultural contexts that urge us to consider our positioning and practice in times of profound collective suffering.

In a review of *The Friendship Bench: How fourteen grandmothers inspired a mental health revolution* by Dixon Chibanda, we get a glimpse of this inspiring project that was created against the backdrop of a national crisis in Zimbabwe. Through dialogue and reflection, they developed what they call "a philosophy of care", grounded in three steps: *kuvhura pfungwa* (to open the mind), *kusimudzira* (to uplift), and *kusimbisa* (to strengthen). These practices privilege Indigenous knowledge holders over professional expertise, linking stories of suffering to peer support and economic action.

At its heart, *Radiance in Pain and Resilience: The global reverberation of Palestinian historical trauma* by Samah Jabr is about witnessing. But witnessing that has to be done in particular ways. Dr Jabr urges, "Palestinians need the solidarity of others who recognize us as active subjects and fighters for freedom, not as bleeding victims". Here, the historical concept of *Sumud*, often symbolised by the deep roots of an olive tree, becomes a metaphor for steadfastness and endurance, centring solidarity, accountability and community healing. The invitation is clear: "to become witnesses who resist erasure, who join in solidarity, and who help rescue our shared humanity from the rubble of Gaza."

White supremacist groups are on the rise across the world. In Australia, they are now serving as role models for fascists elsewhere, particularly in how they recruit young white men who are struggling. Jason Stanley's *How Fascism Works: The politics of us and them* offers a critical frame for these times. For narrative practitioners, the implications are profound. "As narrative practitioners, when we are working with the stories of people's lives, we are in some ways social historians and cultural workers. We make links across time and across generations. A skill of dignity in the present might be linked to a grandmother's pride, which in turn might be linked to life during World War II or the Depression." We are left with the question – how do we refuse to normalise what was once unthinkable?

Kuvhura pfungwa, kusimudzira, kusimbisa to you, dear reader.

In solidarity
Shelja Sen

ABOUT THE EDITOR

Shelja Sen is narrative therapist, writer and co-founder of Children First, New Delhi. Her latest book is Reclaim Your Life *and she is also a columnist with a national newspaper,* Indian Express. *Shelja has worked as a narrative practitioner and teacher for over 20 years in various contexts in the UK and India. She is an international faculty member at Dulwich Centre Foundation, Adelaide, and a clinical tutor at The University of Melbourne, Australia. Shelja is a curator of the unique skills, expertise and know-how of the children, young people and families she has the honour of working with, and is committed to building innovative, culturally aligned, ethical practices using a feminist intersectional lens.*

Sen, S. (2025). Editorial. *International Journal of Narrative Therapy and Community Work*, (2), i–iii. https://doi.org/10.4320/LUMY4326

Author pronouns: she/her

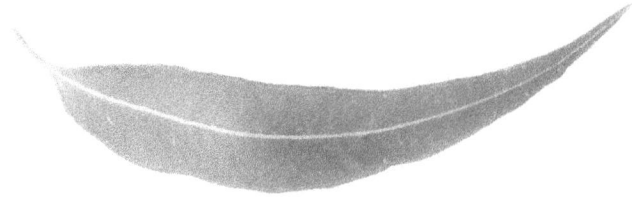

Contents

Reviews

Video

Audio practice note

From the archive

Peer-reviewed papers

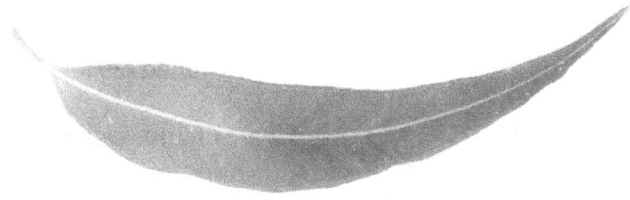

Exploring narrative therapy and therapeutic letter writing in a genetic counselling context

by Stephanie Badman

Stephanie Badman lives and works on Ngunnawal Country in Canberra, Australia. She works as a genetic counsellor at the ACT Genetic Service. Stephanie completed the Master of Narrative Therapy and Community Work at The University of Melbourne in 2024. stephanie.badman@gmail.com

ORCID ID: https://orcid.org/0000-0002-5264-2940

Abstract

This paper explores using narrative therapy in a genetic counselling context to support people having predictive genetic testing for neurogenetic conditions. Using case examples, I describe my use of narrative therapy practices in this setting, with a particular focus on therapeutic letter writing. I set out the ideas from narrative therapy that I considered in the development of my letter-writing practice.

Key words: genetic counselling; genetic counseling; genetic; medical; neurodegenerative; neurogenetic; letter writing; narrative therapy; narrative practice

Badman, S. (2025). Exploring narrative therapy and therapeutic letter writing in a genetic counselling context. *International Journal of Narrative Therapy and Community Work*, (2), 1–10. https://doi.org/10.4320/LBZM5098

Author pronouns: she/her

Genetic counselling

I work as a genetic counsellor in a public hospital clinical genetic service. Genetic counselling has been described as "the process of helping people understand and adapt to the medical, psychological and familial implications of genetic contributions to disease" (Resta et al., 2006, p. 77). My work involves meeting with people who are seeking information, support or genetic testing in a variety of contexts across prenatal, paediatric and adult medicine. I work in a team with other genetic counsellors, clinical geneticists (medical specialists) and administrative staff. Genetic counselling usually occurs over one to three sessions, although this is flexible depending on individual needs.

Predictive genetic testing for neurogenetic conditions

This paper describes meetings with people who are considering predictive genetic testing for neurogenetic conditions.

Neurogenetic is an umbrella term used to broadly describe genetic conditions that affect the nervous system. These conditions affect the central nervous system (brain and spinal cord) and/or the peripheral nervous system (all the nerves that connect the central nervous system to other body parts). Neurogenetic conditions affect the ways people move, think, behave, communicate and relate to others. Many neurogenetic conditions are progressive, meaning they become worse with time and result in early death. Other neurogenetic conditions progress slowly or are more stable over a person's lifetime. There are very few treatments or preventative measures for neurogenetic conditions. Some examples are Huntington disease, motor neurone disease, frontotemporal dementia, spinocerebellar ataxias, neuropathies, myotonic dystrophy and the muscular dystrophies[1] (Crook et al., 2022; Goldman, 2014).

Neurogenetic conditions have profound effects on families because they can be inherited and passed from one generation to the next. A feature of some neurogenetic conditions is that they can cause more significant symptoms and have an earlier age of onset in subsequent generations of a family. For example, myotonic dystrophy can cause symptoms later in life (after the age of 50) for some people. The specific gene fault can then "expand", causing subsequent generations to develop symptoms in early adulthood, childhood or from birth (congenital myotonic dystrophy) (Goldman, 2014).

Predictive genetic testing is for people who are at risk of developing a genetic condition but currently have no symptoms (Crook et al., 2022).[2] For example, a person may have a parent with Huntington disease and want to know if they have inherited the condition. If they have inherited the condition, they will very likely develop symptoms in their lifetime. People seek testing for varied reasons and at different life stages. Predictive testing can help people plan how to have children of their own, particularly if they want to avoid passing the condition on to future generations. Testing can also help people make plans for their life, such as buying an accessible house or deciding on a career that could accommodate early symptoms of the condition. Genetic testing is undertaken in a genetics laboratory using a blood sample.

Genetic counselling involves consideration of the genetic, medical, social, reproductive and financial implications of predictive testing (Crook et al., 2022; MacLeod et al., 2013). It includes counselling to support decision-making about whether to have testing, and consideration of the ways people hope to be supported through the process. If a person decides to proceed with testing, they need to formally consent to the test.

Operations of power

Genetic counselling is a mandatory requirement of predictive genetic testing, with established protocols and guidelines that support this process (Crook et al., 2022; MacLeod et al., 2013). The aims of genetic counselling are to enable informed consent and to support psychological wellbeing and safety. Although these aims are important, people seeking genetic testing sometimes question the value and purpose of genetic counselling. Narrative practice has led me to explore these concerns with the people I am meeting with, and to reflect on the operations of power that support my position as a health care professional in this process:

- Some people find the process of genetic counselling frustrating or unhelpful. They have said things like, "I've already made my decision. Why can't I just have the test?" or "This counselling isn't helpful for me; it makes things more difficult than just dealing with the result". These statements are commonly made by people caring for a family member affected by the condition, or by those who have already been considering their decision about genetic testing for months or years.

- It takes several months to obtain a referral, wait for appointments and receive a genetic test result. People tell me this waiting time is difficult, and they feel a lack of control over the process.

- The requirement to undertake genetic counselling places me in a "gatekeeper" role within the system. It also invites ideas about approval or assessment: people can feel they need to demonstrate their suitability to undertake predictive testing. This can lead them to wonder if they are being observed and evaluated, and to adjust their behaviour accordingly (White, 2016).

- The medical setting is one that privileges professional knowledge over local non-expert knowledge. As a holder of professional knowledge in this system, I carry the power that comes with this expert position. The significant local knowledges of the people I am meeting with can be devalued in this context.

I have found the postmodern approach and values of narrative practice to be supportive in guiding my responses to the operations of power in this setting by:

- drawing attention to systemic harms and injustice

- working in ways that promote justice

- attending to the effects of power and privilege

- respecting and valuing people's own local knowledge and skills.

Introducing narrative therapy to genetic counselling

As I have learnt more about narrative therapy, I have adjusted the way I approach genetic counselling for people considering predictive genetic testing.

Key methods and practices I have been using include:

- externalising conversations (White, 2007) to explore the impacts of genetic conditions on people's lives and families, and the impacts of the predictive testing process

- re-authoring conversations (Carey & Russell, 2003; White, 2007) to explore people's choices about testing, and the hopes, values and commitments that inform these choices

- re-membering conversations (Hedtke, 2014; Russell & Carey, 2002) to explore significant support figures and relationships in people's lives

- ideas about folk psychology and the value of local non-expert knowledge (Freedman & Combs, 1996; White, 2004) to explore people's skills and knowhow for getting through the testing process and coping with test results.

I noticed this approach was helpful in supporting people to create a "riverbank position" from which to embark on genetic testing. The riverbank metaphor was coined by Caleb Wakhungu to describe the use of narrative techniques to create a "different territory of identity", built upon preferred storylines, to support children who have experienced trauma. The riverbank is "a safe place to stand" without being "swept along by the current" (White, 2006, p. 89). I have been using narrative therapy to help people create a riverbank position that is supportive throughout the process of genetic testing. These conversations are underpinned by an assumption that lives are multi-storied, and a commitment to linking current choices about genetic testing to broader hopes, values and commitments which have a history in people's lives. My use of narrative practices in a genetic counselling context has been significantly influenced by the work of MacLeod et al. (2021), Stopford et al. (2020) and Ferrer-Duch (2025), who have introduced narrative practice to genetic counselling and reflective supervision for genetic counsellors.

Narrative conversations facilitate a "thickening" of the plot of preferred storylines (Carey & Russell, 2003), which I feel increases resilience as people move through a predictive genetic testing process. With this new approach, I noticed counselling conversations became more grounded in the specific details of people's day-to-day lives. I also noticed that people described their reasons for testing and their knowhow for getting through the process in ways that became more diverse and distinctive, rather than broadly similar. However, when I shared test results with people, it was often hard for them to remain in touch with their preferred storylines. This was especially noticeable if the genetic testing results returned unwanted news (often showing a person had inherited the condition in their family). In this situation, the shock of results can be destabilising. It is hard to remain in touch with hopes, values and knowhow, and local knowledges are easily displaced.

It was in this context that I began to think about the possibilities of therapeutic letter writing to record and make more secure people's preferred storylines: their hopes and reasons for testing, the values that support these hopes, their skills and knowhow, and the support figures in their lives.

Therapeutic documentation in narrative practice

There is a rich history of therapeutic documentation in narrative therapy, including various kinds of letters, poems, certificates and drawings that act as records of preferred identities and storylines that emerge in therapy (Madigan, 2011; Nylund & Thomas, 1994; White & Epston, 1990). More than recordkeeping, therapeutic documents create possibilities for the witnessing and re-witnessing of preferred identities (Carlson, 2020; Myerhoff, 1986). The letters I started writing were:

- material evidence of my act of witnessing and authenticating the preferred identities of people I was meeting with

- a document through which people could witness themselves as they made decisions to undertake or decline genetic testing

- an opportunity for reflexive re-witnessing (and potentially revising) of preferred identities after genetic test results are known.

The letters allowed people to be actors and audiences (Myerhoff, 1986) or "insiders" and "outsiders" (Carlson, 2020) to their own emerging stories and preferred identities.

In constructing the letters, I tried to capture the essence of our conversations and what was important to people as they undertook genetic testing. I also thought about

the act of "rescuing" aspects of the conversations which might be easily forgotten (Newman, 2008). This has a particular relevance to genetic counselling where psychosocial counselling is interwoven with an exchange of medical and genetic information. In this context it is easy for descriptions of hopes, values, acts of support, skills and commitments to be lost in a sea of professionalised "expert" knowledge, combined with grief and worry about genetic test results. Letter writing is part of my commitment to secure these non-expert local knowledges, and to witness and authenticate people's preferred identity claims as they undertake genetic counselling and testing.

I will share some stories of practice through themes that emerged from my work with three people who decided to proceed with genetic counselling.[3]

Hopes and values

I have found narrative practice particularly helpful to support people in exploring their reasons for having genetic testing and their hopes for how the genetic test result could support their preferred ways of living. The re-authoring conversations maps (Carey & Russell, 2003; White, 2007) were integral to these conversations. I learnt to ask scaffolding questions that help people link their decisions about testing (landscape of action) to their hopes and values for living (landscape of identity), and consider what actions they could take in response to different genetic test results (landscape of action). I have noticed these conversations lead to richer understandings of people's reasons for choosing to have testing, and this is supportive of them when they receive test results. If the result returns difficult news, reflection on people's reasons for testing, and the values that underpin these reasons, can be grounding. I have outlined my approach to re-authoring conversations in Figure 1.

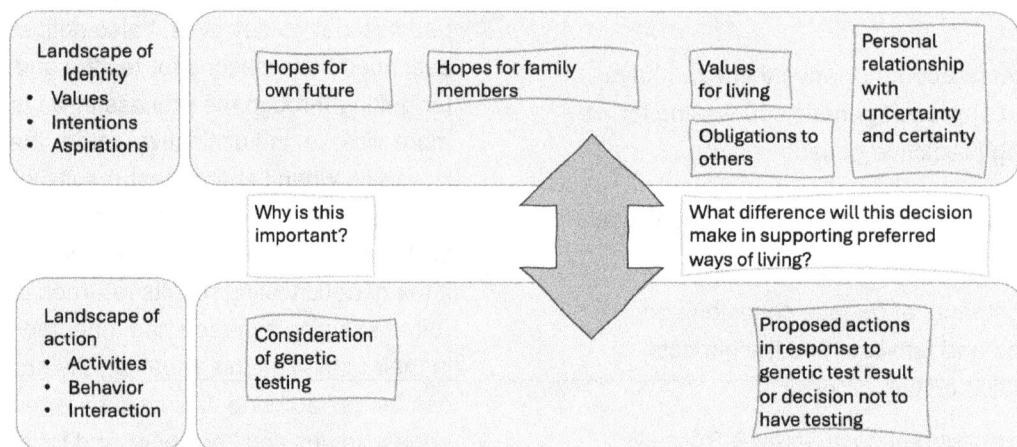

Figure 1: Re-authoring conversations map to explore reasons for undertaking predictive genetic testing.

Nathan

I met with Nathan and his partner, Kate. One of Nathan's parents had recently been diagnosed with a neurogenetic condition, and Nathan had a 50% chance of inheriting the condition from them. Nathan and Kate had a young child who was born before they had knowledge of the neurogenetic condition in his family. Nathan's reason for testing was directly linked to his hope for another baby, and a value about not passing on a serious genetic condition to the next generation. If Nathan's test result was positive, he and Kate planned to use IVF to conceive a second pregnancy that would not inherit the condition.

Some of the questions I asked Nathan were:

- Why is it important for you to know this information before you have another baby? Is this linked to something you value?

- Who are you thinking of in your decision to have this test?

- What do you want to remember about what's important when your genetic test results come back?

- What might be your next step if your genetic test result is positive [or negative]?

Excerpt from Nathan's letter

You told me one of your main reasons to have genetic testing was related to you and Kate wanting to have another baby. Now that you know [neurogenetic condition] is in your family, you said, "I don't want to keep it passing down the family line … we should try and stop it now when we can".

…

You said that you wanted to take this one step at a time. The most immediate thing in front of you and Kate is your hope to have another baby, and a desire not to pass [neurodegenerative condition] on to them. You told me, "For now, I'm just thinking of the next generations".

…

I asked you if there's anything you'd like to remember for yourself when the results come back. You told me: "I'd be pretty upset to think that [our child] could have [the condition]. But there are ways to help situations … it's not like it's the end of the world. We need to look at it in a positive way, as much as we can. There's treatments and IVF. Nothing's going to stop life. Moving forward is important for us. I don't want to stop that; it's just the ways that we'll do it, I guess".

Lou

I met with Lou, an Aboriginal woman aged in her 30s who had young children. Lou was seeking predictive genetic testing for the neurogenetic condition in her family. Her decision to have genetic testing was related to "healing" and "learning to face up to difficult things". Lou described a multigenerational history of hardship in her family, some of which was related to colonial violence and the trauma that resulted from this. Lou was advocating for her kids to have more opportunities and support than she did when she was at school.

Excerpt from Lou's letter

You told me having testing would be part of healing, of learning to face up to feelings and difficult things. You told me you wanted to stop blocking things out.

You also told me how you are learning to stop pretending things are okay. You said [your son] always knows if you are upset or struggling with something, and he asks if you are okay. Sometimes you shut these enquiries down, and other times you're able to tell him something is wrong. I wonder what it means to you that he notices you and is curious about how you are going. How do you think he learnt these skills? You told me you want to be a good example and help your boys learn to talk and share their feelings. You told me you want to break the cycle of difficult communication in your family, and you think this could have a big impact for your boys.

Skills and knowhow

An important part of pre-test genetic counselling is exploring the resources and support people have for coping with the genetic testing process and results. This part of my genetic counselling practice has developed significantly with narrative therapy ideas. Previously I would have asked in general terms about a person's close family and friends, professional psychological supports, and ways of coping. With narrative practice I have begun to ask questions that invite people to describe their own skills and knowhow in rich and particular ways. The re-authoring conversations maps (Carey & Russell, 2003; White, 2007) have guided me during these conversations, leading me to enquire about the values, significance and histories of people's skills and knowhow. I have noticed the conversations are increasingly centred in the lives and knowledge of the people I am meeting with.

Some of the questions I have asked are:

- Have you experienced any hard times in the past?

- What kinds of things did you find yourself doing that helped?

- When did you first start doing these things? How did you learn these skills? Were they introduced to you by someone?

- Why is it important to you to maintain these routines/skills/activities?

Excerpt from Nathan's letter

We talked about some of the things you do when things get tough, and which could be useful to remember after your result comes through.

You told me how you like to go fishing, and that this is a good way to spend quiet time with yourself. You said that this is not about "running away from problems" but more about "taking time to be positive" and think things through. You told me it's sometimes hard to find the time for this when life is busy, but you thought it would be something to focus on if you need to. You said you don't need to go far to fish, even just a spot at the lake close to home can be nice.

You also told me how you like to be around other people, and this helps to switch off from stressful things. You use this as a way to "leave work stress at work and not take anything home".

You said you have a couple of [sport] trips booked in with your friends. You also said you and your friends like helping each other with work on your houses. There is someone in every trade, so you can join together and get things done.

You said it's a balance, spending time by yourself and also keeping busy and being around other people.

This excerpt from Nathan's letter demonstrates how I was able to scaffold a conversation around his love of fishing. Nathan described this as important because it allowed him to "take time to be positive". The letter also makes visible some of the barriers for Nathan in being able to fish, and his strategies for overcoming these barriers.

Acts of support

Another important aspect of genetic counselling for predictive testing is exploring the social, family and/or professional support people have in their lives. In the past I have found it easy for conversations to become focused on "psychological safety" and making sure the people I am working with have access to appropriate professional support. While this is important, narrative practice has given me tools to explore the support people have in ways that are more embedded in their day-to-day life. I am increasingly on the lookout for less visible connections or acts of support, rather than psychological or social "problems".

I have drawn heavily on the narrative practice of re-membering for these conversations about supportive figures and actions of support people are receiving as they undertake genetic testing (Hedtke, 2014; Russell & Carey, 2002). Re-membering was described by Myerhoff (1982, p. 111) as a "special type of recollection" that allows people to purposefully reorganise the membership of their support system. Re-membering conversations provide possibilities for thinking of support more broadly and placing that support within a historical and social context that is supportive of people's preferred identities.

Some questions I have asked are:

- Is there someone in your life who would be supportive of you having this testing [even if they don't know you are here]?

- Is there something they do [or say] that lets you know they are/would support you?

- What impact do these words [or actions] have on you?

- Why do you think it would be important to them to offer this support?

- What do you think it would mean to them, to know that you are leaning on them for support?

Excerpt from Nathan's letter

> You told me about how Kate and your family are wonderful supports. I could see how Kate supported you when she came to the first genetics appointment with you. I remember her saying that it was your choice whether to have testing, and that she would support you either way. What difference does it make to you that she is supporting you in this way? You also said it's made a difference that you've been able to talk with Kate about IVF, and how you might work together towards having another baby. You said these conversations have made you feel like "it will be okay".
>
> You told me about how your friends have been checking in and making sure you're okay as you move through this genetic testing process. You told me it's been good to share a little bit about [neurogenetic condition] and the testing with them. They let you know they support you by saying things like "I hope everything's going to be okay" or by asking about when your appointments are or how they went.

This excerpt from Nathan's letter documents the support his friends provide by checking in with him. Nathan wasn't forthcoming with details about his friends or other supports, but by "rescuing" the few things he did say about this, I was able to capture these ideas and fix them in text. I hoped this would be a reminder to Nathan, capturing something brief that might be otherwise forgotten among the other things we discussed. It also created a stepping stone – a base of understanding that we could return to in a future session if we needed to.

In Nathan's letter I also included some of my own reflections about Kate's support. I did this because Nathan and I didn't have an opportunity to explore Kate's support in detail together. I wanted to keep the letter as close to Nathan's own words and responses

as possible, and clearly state the difference between my observations and his words. I hoped this distinction would make it easier for Nathan to disregard my interpretation of Kate's support if it didn't resonate with him.

Lou

In conversation with Lou, I drew on the re-membering conversations map (White, 2007) to connect her ways of coping in hard times with the significant people in her life. This led to some beautiful and unexpected reflections on Lou's relationship with each of her parents. Lou shared that going and having a cup of tea with her mum would be comforting. When I enquired about this further, Lou told me their relationship had been difficult in the years previously, but they had done a lot of work together to improve the relationship. I enquired about the impact of Lou reaching out to her mum for support.

Steph: What do you think it would mean to your mum if you went to her for support?

Lou: I think it would make her feel valued as a mum.

In Lou's case, both her parents were supportive, but in different and incomplete ways. I chose to document the specific ways her parents were helpful in their own ways. My hope was that this might capture the variety of support Lou was receiving from different family members; perhaps this could be considered "multi-storied" support.

Excerpt from Lou's letter

> You also told me about some of the ways you could support yourself after you get your genetic test result. I wonder if some of these ideas could also help while you wait for the testing to be done. Some of the things you mentioned were:
>
> - Hugging your boys.
>
> - Jumping on the trampoline with your boys.
>
> - Ringing your mum. Asking her to have a cuppa or to come over to your place. You told me how your relationship with your mum has improved in the last few years. You said it means a lot to you that she's there to support you, and you think it would make her feel valued as a mum if you reached out to her for support.

- Going to [café] with [your partner] for coffee. You told me this was one of the first cafés you found together when you moved to the area. You enjoy the coffee there, and the staff have got to know you both over time. It's a familiar place.

- Calling your dad for a chat. You told me there are some things that he's really good to talk to about. For some of these things, you said he's less judgemental than other people. You also told me he's good at practical support – like coming for a sleepover with your boys so you and [your partner] can have a night out together. You told me your dad often says how proud he is of you. You think this is because you're being proactive about doing things in your life to support your family.

Responses to genetic test results

It is not unusual for people who receive a negative genetic test result (meaning they have not inherited the condition) to experience some distress, despite receiving the result they were hoping for (MacLeod et al., 2018). This can be related to shock or disbelief, changes in self-perception, reactions from family members, or a feeling of guilt at being dealt "a good hand" when others in the family had been less lucky.

Dan

Dan's response to his "good news" genetic test result was quite profound, and this led me to write him a letter that "rescued" what I could of his response to the result. This was a particularly tender appointment, and I didn't feel it was respectful to record or take too many notes as we were talking. For this reason, the letter contains fewer direct quotes, instead focusing on my attempt to capture the meaning of Dan's story. Dan told me he was so shocked by the genetic test result that he couldn't imagine what was next for him in life; he'd had a rough and traumatic past, and this result felt like one of the only times something had gone well. In our conversation, I focused on asking questions that allowed Dan to connect actions and commitments from his earlier life to his hopes for the future. Re-membering practices allowed Dan to reconnect himself to his sister and nephew, his hopes for their future, and the part he could play in this.

Excerpt from Dan's letter

You said you didn't allow yourself to think the result could be negative for [neurogenetic condition]. You said it's one of the first times in life when something important hasn't gone badly for you; it was actually a really big shock to receive the result.

You told me how much Harry [nephew] means to you, and how he has brought you closer to Louise [sister]. You talked about being a good uncle for Harry, and how this result means you'll be able to support Louise when she develops [neurogenetic condition].

You told me all about your interest in astronomy, and how you're clever at maths. You told me how you like to learn about space and stars and other astronomy things using YouTube. Even though it's difficult to do a lot of things because of your back injury, you're still able to keep learning. You said this is because of your curiosity about the universe and how it works. I'm wondering if one day you might get the chance to share some of this knowledge with Harry.

You also said you wanted to learn to fly a helicopter, and talked about the simulated training centre in [suburb]. You said this is something on your bucket list, and something that might be possible now you know you won't develop [neurogenetic condition]. Maybe some other things will be possible too?

Negotiating letters

An aspect of letter writing I am still working on is having careful and thorough discussions with people about whether they would like to receive a letter, and what would be most relevant to include in the letter.

The times when I have asked people what they would like me to include in a letter have been quite revealing. When I asked Nathan if there was anything he would like me to write down for him to remember when the results come back, he said,

I'd be pretty upset to think that [my son] could have something. But there are ways to help situations … it's not like it's the end of the world. We need to look at it in a positive way, as much as we can. There's treatments and IVF. Nothing's going to stop life .... moving forward is important for us. I don't want to stop that; it's just the ways that we'll do it, I guess.

To me, this seemed like Nathan had crystallised what was most important in the testing.

There have also been many times when my attempts at negotiating letters led to indifferent responses, with people saying things like "Sure, that's okay", or "Yeah, you can do that". As I move forward with this work, it may help to share an example of a therapeutic letter with people, so they can have a sense of what I am thinking about and whether this is of interest to them.

It may also be that some more interesting questions are needed to get a real sense of what would be useful for people:

- Is there anything you would not want me to include in the letter?

- If you were writing a letter to yourself to capture what was important, what would you want to include?

- When do you think the letter would be most useful to receive?

- Do you think it would be useful to share this kind of letter with anyone?

Sharing letters

Some of my biggest learnings have come from sharing letters with people. I have shared several therapeutic letters with people during their results appointment and found they were not able to fully engage with the letters in that moment. My observation has been that the impact of the result is significant, and people haven't had capacity to engage with anything additional.

As an alternative, I sent Lou's letter to her by email in the period between having DNA samples collected for the test and receiving the result (this is usually about two months). During Lou's results appointment, we reread the letter together, and Lou told me she had been drawing on some of the skills and support actions mentioned in the letter during the weeks she was waiting for her result. Ideas in the letter, such as Lou's larger project of "healing" and "learning to face up to difficult things", then became themes in future sessions we had together as her child subsequently had genetic testing. From my position, this project of *healing*, which was made "more solid" in the therapeutic letter, gave us a broader purpose for future genetic counselling with her child. There was a shift from focusing on the result as a binary (positive or negative for the condition), to focusing on *healing* regardless of the result. In this sense, either result was manageable for Lou, because both could be supportive of healing and caring for her children.

These observations have led me to believe it is better to share supportive letters with people in the time after their DNA samples are collected, and before the results are available. This gives people a chance to read and engage with the letter on their own terms, so it might be drawn on as a familiar and supportive resource after they receive their test result.

Notes

[1] Some of these conditions also have non-genetic causes.

[2] This is distinct from diagnostic testing, which is genetic testing for a person who has clinical symptoms of a suspected genetic condition.

[3] All participants have expressed willingness and provided consent for our work together to be included in this paper. I have used pseudonyms and removed identifying details. I would like to share my gratitude for the participants in this work for their openness and willingness to explore the possibilities of narrative therapy with me.

References

Carey, M., & Russell, S. (2003). Re-authoring: Some answers to commonly asked questions. *International Journal of Narrative Therapy and Community Work*, (3), 60–71.

Carlson, T. S. (2020). Who is the outsider in insider and outsider witnessing practices? Toward a theory of outsight in narrative therapy. *Journal of Narrative Family Therapy*, (1), 46–63.

Crook, A., Jacobs, C., Newton-John, T., O'Shea, R., & McEwen, A. (2022). Genetic counseling and testing practices for late-onset neurodegenerative disease: A systematic review. *Journal of Neurology, 269*(2), 696–692. https://doi.org/10.1007/s00415-021-10461-5

Ferrer-Duch, M. (2025). Collaborative contributions to genetics: Systemic and narrative approaches. *Journal of Family Therapy, 47*(2), e12488. https://doi.org/10.1111/1467-6427.12488

Freedman, J., & Combs, G. (1996). *Narrative therapy*. Norton.

Goldman, J. S. (Ed.). (2014). *Genetic counseling for adult neurogenetic disease: A casebook for clinicians*. Springer.

Hedtke, L. (2014). Creating stories of hope: A narrative approach to illness, death and grief. *Australian and New Zealand Journal of Family Therapy, 35*(1), 4–19. https://doi.org/10.1002/anzf.1040

MacLeod, R., Moldovan, R., Stopford, C., & Ferrer-Duch, M. (2018). Genetic counselling and narrative practices: A model of support following a "negative" predictive test for Huntington's disease. *Journal of Huntington's disease, 7*(2), 175–183. https://doi.org/10.3233/jhd-170276

MacLeod, R., Metcalfe, A., & Ferrer-Duch, M. (2021). A family systems approach to genetic counseling: Development of narrative interventions. *Journal of Genetic Counseling, 30*(1), 22–29. https://doi.org/10.1002/jgc4.1377

MacLeod, R., Tibben, A., Frontali, M., Evers-Kiebooms, G., Jones, A., Martinez-Descales, A., Roos, R. A., & Editorial Committee and Working Group 'Genetic Testing Counselling' of the European Huntington Disease Network. (2013). Recommendations for the predictive genetic test in Huntington's disease. *Clinical Genetics, 83*(3), 221–231. https://doi.org/10.1111/j.1399-0004.2012.01900.x

Madigan, S. (2011). *Narrative therapy*. American Psychological Association.

Myerhoff, B. (1982). Life history among the elderly: Performance, visibility and re-membering. In J. Ruby (Ed.), *A crack in the mirror: Reflective perspectives in anthropology* (pp. 99–117). University of Pennsylvania Press.

Myerhoff, B. (1986). "Life not death in Venice": Its second life. In V. Turner & E. Bruner (Eds.), *The Anthropology of experience* (pp. 261–286). University of Illinois Press.

Newman, D. (2008). "Rescuing the said from the saying of it": Living documentation in narrative therapy. *International Journal of Narrative Therapy and Community Work*, (3), 24–34.

Nylund, D., & Thomas, J. (1994). The economics of narrative. *Family Therapy Networker, 18*(6), 38–39.

Resta, R., Biesecker, B. B., Bennett, R. L., Blum, S., Estabrooks Hahn, S., Strecker, M. N., & Williams, J. L. (2006). A new definition of genetic counseling: National Society of Genetic Counselors' task force report. *Journal of Genetic Counseling, 15*, 77–83. https://doi.org/10.1007/s10897-005-9014-3

Russell, S., & Carey, M. (2002). Re-membering: Responding to commonly asked questions. *International Journal of Narrative Therapy and Community Work*, (3), 23–31.

Stopford, C., Ferrer-Duch, M., Moldovan, R., & MacLeod, R. (2020). Improving follow up after predictive testing in Huntington's disease: Evaluating a genetic counselling narrative group session. *Journal of Community Genetics, 11*(1), 47–58.

White, M. (2004). Folk psychology and narrative practice. In M. White (Ed.), *Narrative practice and exotic lives: Resurrecting diversity in everyday life* (pp, 60–115). Dulwich Centre Publications.

White, M. (2006). Responding to children who have experienced significant trauma: A narrative perspective. In M. White & A. Morgan (Eds.), *Narrative therapy with children and their families* (85–97). Dulwich Centre Publications.

White, M. (2007). *Maps of narrative practice*. Norton.

White, M. (2016). Deconstruction and therapy. In M. White (Ed.), *Narrative therapy classics* (pp. 11–54). Dulwich Centre Publications.

White, M., & Epston, D. (1990). *Narrative means to therapeutic ends*. Norton.

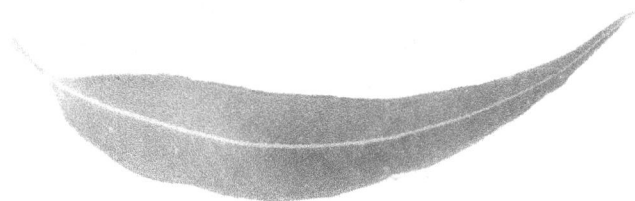

"Love always":

Letters written by dying mothers for their children

by Tanya Newman

Tanya Newman is a hospice social worker in Whangārei, Aotearoa New Zealand. Tanya is Pākehā and lives on the lands of ngā hapū o Whangārei Terenga Parāoa. Her background is in social work lecturing, feminist community organisations, social justice education and union organising. Tanya completed Dulwich Centre's one-year program in narrative therapy and community work in 2024. For Tanya, connecting with narrative ideas and practices felt like a homecoming. She is now a student of the Master of Narrative Therapy and Community Work at The University of Melbourne. Tanya looks forward to extending the ideas and practice shared in this article, particularly in her work with people who are dying or grieving the death of a loved one. emailfortanya@gmail.com

Abstract

This article shares stories of dying mothers writing letters for their children. The author conceives of letter writing as a way for mothers to re-member their preferred identities, and the letters as portals for future re-membering for children. The article includes examples of questions asked in interviews with mothers, the thinking behind the questions, and excerpts from the letters these conversations enabled.

Key words: hospice; palliative care; end of life; death; grief; children; therapeutic documents; letters; re-membering; narrative practice; narrative therapy

Newman, T. (2025). "Love always": Letters written by dying mothers for their children. *International Journal of Narrative Therapy and Community Work*, (2), 11–20. https://doi.org/10.4320/RBKC6395

Author pronouns: she/her

© Tanya Newman. Distributed under the terms of the Creative Commons Attribution-NonCommercial-NoDerivs licence
Published by Dulwich Centre Foundation | www.dulwichcentre.com.au

As a palliative care social worker in Aotearoa New Zealand, I support people in their final months, weeks and days of life. While many hospice patients are 70 or older, we also care for people in their 30s, 40s and 50s, many of whom are parents to young children.

As a mother myself, I was uncertain about whether my heart could cope with caring for dying mothers. I was explicit about this at my job interview, and was reassured that other staff could lead this work. However, this changed the first time I met Tūi[1], a hospice patient close in age to me, with children of a similar age to mine. Tūi was staying in the hospice inpatient unit. I visited her briefly to drop off a needed form. When I said, "Kia ora[2], I'm Tanya, I'm a social worker", she responded by looking me in the eye, sizing me up, and telling me, "You're on my team now". She then added my name to a poster she'd made with the names of her key support people.

Thus began a four-month journey of supporting Tūi and her whānau[3], and my ongoing efforts to support parents nearing death. The time I spent with Tūi expanded my heart and grew my courage. She knew I had a contribution to make, before I knew it myself, and she gave me the push I needed to show up for her, for other young parents, and for their children. The work shared in this article is one thread of Tūi's legacy.

Dying mums are also living mums

The time I spent with Tūi was before I trained in narrative therapy and community work. Narrative practice has offered me further knowledges and skills to bring to the work. My leap into narrative practice coincided with my work with Theresa. Like Tūi, Theresa had the unfinished work of raising children. Theresa's children were devastated about their mother's illness and were having very tough times.

As Theresa shared her concerns with me, she spoke about how hard it was for her son Rowan to be "the kid with a dying mum". I was struck by this single-storied description. In an effort to re-author this dominant storyline, I asked Theresa what she thought about this and offered the idea of also being a "living mum". Her face lit up as she said, "Yes! I am a *living* mum. That's how I want the kids to see me".

In retrospect, I could have asked questions that supported Theresa to explore and define her own alternative storyline(s), rather than offering the idea of being a "living mum". I wonder where such a conversation could have taken us. At the time, I offered

an alternative as I was aware that the identity of "dying mother" was painful for Theresa, her illness meant our conversations were often brief, and I wanted to offer hope. Not hope in the sense of optimism, but a grounded hope that is relational, action oriented and able to hold despair: a "reasonable hope" that helps to "make sense of what exists now in the belief that this prepares us to meet what lies ahead" (Weingarten, 2010, p. 7). However, by inserting my idea of an alternative story, I may have limited Theresa's opportunity to re-author her life in her own words. If I could re-visit the conversation, I might do it differently. However, I'm aware that being a "living mum" was a helpful shift for Theresa. If the idea hadn't been resonant, our conversation would have moved in other directions. Theresa embraced the idea, and our conversations continued from there.

Time spent with Tūi, Theresa and other mums has had me thinking about how dying mums are living, have lived and will live on in their children. They are mums who physically leave, but who also stay in their children's hearts, memories and actions. These ideas have been resonant with the parents I have supported since.

Like others connected with Theresa's children, I was concerned for their wellbeing. I considered offering them my support. This would have been stepping outside my role as their mum's social worker, and outside my organisation's usual approach of supporting adults to support their children. This also would have centred me (Morgan, 2006). What the children wanted was a well mother, not a well-meaning social worker! My role was to support Theresa to give as much of herself to her children as she could, as this was her own priority. Alongside a range of practical steps, this orientation led me to re-membering practices.

Re-membering: Past, present, future

Michael White conceived of re-membering as

> evoke[ing] the image of a person's life and identity as an association or a club. The membership of this association of life is made up of the significant figures of a person's history, as well as the identities of the person's present circumstances, whose voices are influential with regard to how the person constructs his or her own identity. (White, 2007, p. 134)

Given that mothers and children are often influential in shaping one another's identities, this seemed relevant for Theresa and Rowan.

While re-membering practices are commonly used to "support people to reposition themselves in relation to the death of a loved one, in ways that bring relief" (White, 2007, p. 135), I saw the potential for re-membering to assist Theresa and Rowan in reclaiming their preferred sense of themselves, each other and their relationship *before* Theresa died. Indeed, Barbara Myerhoff, who coined the term "re-membering", included "one's own prior selves" as figures that can be re-membered (Myerhoff, 1982, p. 111). I hoped re-membering could extend Rowan's sense of identity beyond "the kid with a dying mum" and strengthen Theresa's reclamation of herself as "a living mum". I also hoped re-membering might support Theresa and Rowan to "say hullo again" to their sense of love and connection with one another (White, 1988).

As I was not working with Rowan, I was challenged to find ways to offer re-membering without meeting him. Aware of Theresa's limited energy, I wanted to work in ways that could maximise her efforts to be a living mum. At the time Theresa and I were meeting, I was experimenting with writing collective documents and had recently read David Newman's (2008) piece "Rescuing the said from the saying of it". I was struck by a sense of ethical obligation to record people's knowledges to hand back to them. I highlighted Newman's sentence "over the years, I have noticed that documentation is regularly a reassuring and generative aspect of my work" (2008, p. 24). As I struggled to work out how I could contribute to Theresa and her children, I was in need of some generative reassurance! I felt both out of my depth and committed to being as useful as possible. So, I turned to narrative documentation and offered to support Theresa to craft a letter for Rowan. I hoped a letter might be useful in the present, offer a portal for future re-membering, and provide a small way for Theresa to live into her son's future.

Letters of love

Theresa accepted my invitation and shared my hope that a letter might support Rowan to reconnect with her as his living mum and with his preferred sense of himself. Theresa liked these ideas very much, particularly the idea that Rowan could continue to re-visit the letter throughout his life. I hoped the letter-writing process might also support Theresa to "re-member" herself as a capable, loving, present mum.

Theresa and I spent an hour together in which I interviewed her about Rowan using re-membering questions. I recorded the conversation and took notes. I will forever remember the impact sharing stories about her son had on Theresa. Her skin brightened, with colour returning to her cheeks. Theresa smiled brightly, and she looked considerably more well. It was a privilege to see how Theresa's love for her son lit her from the inside out. When I think of the value of re-membering, Theresa's glowing face is the image I hold.

Following our interview, I edited the pages of notes into a two-page letter. Due to her deteriorating health, this was not a task Theresa was well enough to do herself, so I leant my energy to the work. I emailed the draft letter to Theresa, saying,

> I've attached a draft of your letter for Rowan. 90%+ of the words are yours. I needed to add some joining words in places, and work with the order of what you shared. Please feel very welcome to change anything that doesn't feel right, whether it's tweaking or rewriting the letter entirely. I'd love your feedback about what works and what doesn't.

She wrote back:

> The letter is perfect, thank you. It brought tears to my eyes. I couldn't ask for anything more for my little man to have as a remembrance of me and my thoughts.

Theresa gave the letter to Rowan. When he read it, he gave Theresa a big hug. Theresa asked that we also write a letter for her daughter, Aria. We repeated the process, and when Theresa received Aria's letter she said:

> Tanya, I can't thank you enough for expressing my love and thoughts to my darling daughter. Thank you, it's perfect.
>
> Lots of gratitude, Theresa x

Theresa died three months after she wrote the letters. I haven't spoken to either of her children, so I don't know how the experience has been for them. However, I witnessed the relief that recording her love in perpetuity brought for Theresa. Both children spoke at Theresa's funeral, and I was moved by the love, care and connection they expressed for their mum.

Dani also chose to work with me to write letters for her kids. Dani's health rapidly declined between writing a letter for her eldest and writing a letter for her youngest a few days later. I am in awe of the determination she showed to ensure she left a letter for her daughter. Dani completed our interview, despite slipping in and out of consciousness. We continued the work, knowing it might be all the time she had. Sadly, we were right. Dani died a few days after finishing her second letter. I hope having the letter read to her helped ease her dying, knowing she had completed this important task.

In the next section, I will share examples of the questions I used when supporting Theresa and Dani to write letters for their children, the thinking behind the questions, and excerpts from the letters they enabled. The questions are grouped into themes and presented in a linear fashion; however, that is an outcome of sharing the work in written form rather than an accurate reflection of the interviews, which were more conversational and organic. I encouraged Theresa and Dani to reject any questions that didn't work for them, and I followed their interests, building on questions they received warmly rather than working through a preprepared script.

Through a mother's loving eyes

I started the interviews with questions that invited descriptions of the children. This was a way to warm up the conversation, with each woman introducing her children to me. Theresa lit up as she spoke, and Dani relaxed into sharing her stories.

The questions included:

- Could you introduce [child] to me?

- What can you tell me about [child]?

- What are some of your best memories of [child]?

- If [child] were to see themselves through your eyes, what would they see?

As Theresa and Dani spoke, I asked for examples to illustrate their points. My hope was this would offer "experience-near" (White, 2007, p. 40) language that the children could relate to, that it would anchor words to shared memories and "thicken" (Morgan, 2000, p. 15) stories beyond platitudes to meaningful identity descriptions the children could connect with. As I drafted the letters, I noticed this meant Theresa's and Dani's words often shifted between landscape of action and landscape of identity (White, 2007, pp. 77–78),

moving from stories about doing things with their children to rich description of the children's identities as seen through their mothers' loving eyes (White, 2007). I hope the content these initial descriptions generated will support the children to construct identity in helpful ways.

Here are some examples of the content generated through these questions:

> You are an amazing kid. You brighten up a room when you come in. It makes me proud, the way you speak up if something's not right. I appreciate how you let others know they are loved by doing kind things and saying "I love you". When I think of the way we say, "I love you", "I love you more!", "No, I love you more!", it makes me smile. I hope I have taught you to love easily and whole heartedly. You are kind and gentle: all the beautiful things that anyone would want in a son. And you give the best hugs. I love sinking into your hugs. They're so big and strong and real.

> I've always loved sharing water with you. It's a together thing we had, a way we connect. I was taking you to swimming lessons from when you were six months old. Swimming with you when you were a baby was a beautiful experience. I enjoyed holding you in water, our skin touching. Before Daisy was born, we'd go to your swimming lesson, swim in the pool together for ages afterwards, and then have a sushi date. I loved our special sushi dates. When you were older, I loved the way that when we were in the pool or ocean, you'd hug and cling to me and hold on tight. Surfing together was fun too – you picked it up really fast! The times I've spent in the water with you are some of my best.

> I love your company. My day brightens when you are in it. When you used to race home from school and try to get home in less than five minutes, I'd look forward to hearing you rush inside to check the time on the microwave. Those are good memories. Lockdown was a good time for me – I enjoyed having the extra time with you and Aria, painting, talking, cooking and not worrying about the outside world. I get a lot of pleasure from being in being in your company and Aria's – talking, watching movies and just being together.

Appreciation: "You are such a cool kid"

I was conscious that while the initial readers of Theresa's and Dani's letters were children, the letters were likely to be revisited again and again. Therefore, I was cognisant of the need for the letters to resonate both with their 10 to 15-year-old readers, and also with those same readers when they are 20, 30, 40, 50+ years old. My hope was that the letters would provide their recipients with a sense over time of belonging to their mothers, and that the record of their mother's voice would encourage positive self-regard. The letters could be portals for future re-membering. With this in mind, I asked questions that could enable Theresa's and Dani's children to know what their mums appreciated about them, what they recognised in their children that others may have missed, and what they valued about their children. My questions included:

- What do you admire about [child]?

- When you think of [child], what are you most proud of?

Again, I asked follow-up questions to generate specificity, encourage experience-near language, and foster movement between landscape of action and landscape of identity. These questions led to the following excerpts:

I admire your intelligence and your dry sense of humour. I'm always impressed about how you can come up with lots of facts and little bits of knowledge, and how you teach me things that I have no idea about. I learn so much from you. I'm amazed how you can read books and recite them back, adding your own thoughts, and how you look up YouTubers and learn different facts and spill them out when we least expect them. I admire your brain – that it can soak up so much information. And the way you can crack a joke and put others at ease.

You are a such a cool kid. You're witty, handsome, talented and smart. I love how you are yourself. When you went to school, I admired how if the teachers told you to draw a tree with a brown trunk, and a blue sky, and green grass, you'd ignore them and just make what you wanted to make. I see your creativity now in your gaming, with the way you love to dive into different worlds and adapt avatars. You are imaginative and eccentric. I love that about you.

You are incredibly smart. You taught yourself to read before you were five. You wanted to know what words said, so you'd ask, "Dad, how do you read this? What does this say?" You'd get sick of waiting to be told, so you just picked it up. Then you'd run into the room and say, "Mum, I can read this!" and read me a whole book! You can learn whatever you want to know.

You are also really kind. I see how you try hard with your sister. Like when we went to TimeZone and Daisy didn't have enough credit to pay for the key chain she wanted, so you just went and got it for her. You do stuff like that all the time. I love that you look out for Daisy, and I'm proud of your kindness.

Contribution: "Being your Mum absolutely made me"

Michael White highlighted the mutual contributions people make to one another's lives, and how re-membering practices can offer space to uncover and acknowledge such contributions. Inquiry about contribution is central to the re-membering map of practice (White, 2007).

In the context of parents writing to their children, I think questions about mutual contributions are particularly important. Dominant discourses focus on children being shaped by their parents, and on parents bestowing knowledge, values and skills to their children. Therefore, I was keen to record the contributions that Theresa's and Dani's children had made to the lives of their mothers.

These questions invited some of the most heartfelt replies.

- How has [child] contributed to your life?

- What have you learnt from [child]?

- In what ways has being [child's] mum contributed to your life?

- What does it mean for you to be [child's] mum?

The letters documented some of the contributions Theresa's and Dani's children made to their mothers' lives:

I appreciate the ways you've chilled me out. I've learnt to be much more patient and understanding. I can be quite a high-strung, anxious mum, and you've really supported me in that. I remember a time when I was doing something creative in the art room, and the house was a mess. I got completely overwhelmed and you were like, "Mum, don't worry about the mess, do what you're doing". Thank you. I needed that permission. You told me, "You've done so well, Mum". You are a real sweetheart. You make an amazing son, that's for sure.

Thank you for looking out for me and getting Dad for me when I've needed help.

When I was younger, I was told that I wouldn't be able to have children, so having you and Aria was such a wonderful surprise. I had never thought that I was born to be a mum. But I was. Being your mum absolutely made me. You came into my life and gave me purpose and so much happiness. Once I had you and Aria, it just made sense. This is what my life was meant to be. Being your mum.

Being yours and Daisy's mum is a privilege. I love being in our family. Our family is my home.

Thank you for all of your help. For caring for your brother, and for helping around the house, and for cooking meals. You're a wonderful help, and you do it all while spreading, love, joy, happiness and laughter. Thank you.

My heart got bigger when I became your mum. Everything changed when I had you. You were this beautiful little human being that we somehow had to look after and get to know. My love for you and Daisy is intense and it's unconditional. I'd do anything for you, and I'm proud of you, no matter what!

I love our talks. They are my best times. I love that you share things with me, and that nothing's too shocking to share (even when it is shocking). I've tried to keep things open and nonjudgemental between us. I'm glad you talk to me, and that we've always talked and been open with each other. Let's keep talking.

Skills for living: "You've made it through"

Given the children were already living with a very unwell mother, and that in their near future they would be traversing their mother's death, I was interested in what Theresa and Dani knew about the skills their children had in navigating hard times. I hoped their answers might support the children to resist the collapsing of their identities into "kids whose mum died", and support them to hold on to preferred and useful stories. Questions to thicken stories about their children getting through tough times included:

- What else have you seen [child] overcome in life?

- What skills and knowledges do you think [child] has, that help them get through hard times?

- How do you know this about them?

- Can you tell me a story about [child] when they have shown these skills?

Theresa's and Dani's children had many skills in navigating hard times:

Watching your determination makes me proud. You've made it through hard times, like when our family changed, and you really missed Tom.

We're different from other families, which hasn't always been easy. As a family, we've had to deep dive into learning about our differences and figuring out what works for us. You had it tough with bullying, and I admire your strength in working through that.

Seeing you know what you want and how you stand up for yourself is reassuring for me. I see you stand up for yourself – with me, with your dad, and in the stories you tell me from school. I couldn't be prouder.

You choose people well. I want you to keep listening to your intuition and making good decisions. You have good judgement, which gives me confidence that you'll always be okay. I appreciate that you surround yourself with good people and that you accept help from people that you trust. Keep doing that.

You're going through a lot, and you're doing wonderfully. I'm tremendously proud of you. Be easy on yourself. Don't worry about the future, or about your grades, or about whether you're going to cope. You are stronger than you know. I see your strength every day, in your choices and decisions. You are going to be okay.

The C word

As mentioned previously, Theresa, Dani and I were all conscious of their letters being documents that would be read in the present context and re-read across time. Considering this, I wondered what it might be useful for the children to know about how their mothers made sense of their illness, death and dying. I offered Theresa and Dani an opportunity to share their thoughts about cancer and about dying. I asked:

- What would you like [child] to know about your sickness? Is there anything you want to say to them about death and dying?

They answered:

I know things haven't been the same since we found out the sickness is terminal. It's *really* hard. I'm here, and I want to support you. I want to soak up our time together, for however long we have. I can't walk up hills or go on big adventures anymore, but I am here. I love all the small moments of nurturing that I can do – getting your clothes ready when you get out of the shower, preparing your meals, those simple motherly things mean a lot to me. I love your company. Just being together and having cuddles makes me so happy.

Cancer is so hard. I wish it was different. I didn't want you and Daisy to be witnesses of my suffering, and I'm sorry this is part of your life too. I want you to know that while I'm in pain, I am managing it. It's alright. You don't need to worry about me. Even if I'm hurting, our time together is precious for me. I want to keep having as many family experiences as we can.

I'm so sorry that the cancer has changed your life. I feel a lot of shame about all the hard stuff that is happening for you and Rowan because of the cancer. If I could change it, I would. I wish I could. I'd give anything to protect you from this.

I know the cancer is hard and it's scary. It means the world to me that we can keep letting our love in. Please don't be too scared to love me. I'm here now. Let's be scared and love each other anyway.

My wish for you is a happy life

Thinking of letters as portals for future re-membering, and as a way for mothers' voices to be present in children's lives over time, had me asking what Theresa and Dani might like to say to their children when they are older. I asked questions like:

- What are your hopes and wishes for [child's] future?

- Is there anything you want to share with [child], about being an adult? About being a parent? Any key pieces of advice you want to share?

They answered:

I hope you get to be a dad one day. If you do, I hope you get as much joy out of being a parent as I do! My biggest wish for you is to have happiness. I hope you find a passion, and work on it on a daily basis. I hope your life is as filled with love as mine.

My wish for you is a happy life. A life where you are surrounded by love, which is what you deserve. I hope you are passionate about whatever you choose in life, and that you carry on sharing your joy. Don't worry about the small stuff. Continue to be you, and follow your own path. I know you'll be a wonderful mum one day. When you are, enjoy the moments. It all goes so quickly.

You are an amazing think-outside-the-box person. My main hope is that you create a life for yourself where you thrive, enjoy yourself, and where you can be creative and just be you. The jobs you do in the future may not even have been invented yet. You and Daisy don't fit boxes, so we need to smash out of the box. You're good at that. It suits you.

You've always been the one to look after someone who is a bit different, to take them under your wing. You've always done that, right from preschool. I want you to hold on to that, to continue being kind and to keep finding joy with people. Helping others has been my passion in life, and I see that same caring in you. I'm proud of your kind heart.

"Love always, Mum"

As we reached the end of the letter-writing conversations, I followed Theresa's and Dani's direction. I asked, "What else is there to say?", and they said the most important things:

> I hope these words can help sustain you over time and that they remind you of our connection if I ever feel far away.

> I have a very deep love for you. I am so proud that you are my son. I'd do anything for you and your sister, and you have made that easy. You are an easy person to love.

> I want you to know that I love you, and I will never stop. I will always be there. My physical body will leave, but my energy won't. I'm always going to be hanging around.

> Know that you always belong, and you are always loved. You will always belong with me, Dad and Daisy. The three of you are an amazing team, and you're going to be just fine.

> Please look after Dad. He'll keep going and going, and he's not very good at taking breaks, so you might need to remind him sometimes.

> Trust yourself. Be true to yourself. And know that I love you bigger than words can explain. It's absolutely a pleasure and a privilege to be your mum!

> I love you fiercely, totally and completely. I adore you. I hope you always feel that, with every fibre of your being.

> I will always love you, no matter what. I will always be your mum.

Linking lives: The beginning of an archive

It was a privilege to support Theresa and Dani. I'm grateful for all they taught me. Our work together continues to inform my practice (and my parenting!).

Dying parents have shared with me that they feel alone in the experience. While it is difficult to link lives and build community between hospice patients (due to their limited energy and limited time), Theresa generously agreed to share anonymised copies of her children's letters with other parents who are considering writing to their children. In Theresa's words,

> I'm more than happy for you to share the letters. I'm just so sad and sorry that another young person is going through this journey. I found the letters a wonderful expression of love for my children that they will have there to remind them of my love for them and the special moments we shared.

Theresa's generous contribution in sharing her letters has enabled other parents (including Dani) to feel less alone in their experience and more able to write letters to their own children. My invitation for letters to be shared was inspired by collective narrative practice, and was an effort to link lives and enable those I support to "speak through me, not just to me" (Denborough, 2018, p. 2). In the tradition of David Epston (Epston & White, 1990; see Denborough, 2018, p. 185–186), sharing letters enables dying parents to offer their experience, wisdom and support to others. Dani's husband has given posthumous permission for Dani's letters to also be shared with other parents considering writing letters of their own. Together, Theresa's and Dani's letters are the beginning of an archive

Limitations of the work

The work shared in this article speaks only to my experience supporting the people whose stories I have included. My focus has been on supporting mothers, as they are the people who have invited me into their lives. I recently started working with fathers, and I look forward to learning from these collaborations. While this work endeavours to be child-focused, it has been led by adults. I look forward to learning from children's feedback and to growing my accountability to those with insider knowledge.

Theresa, Dani and I are Pākehā.[4] Written documentation, particularly supported by a Pākehā professional, may be less culturally resonant for Māori. Offers of letter-writing support have not yet been taken up by Māori. This may be for a multitude of reasons (and I'm conscious the sample size is small). However, I have noted a contrast with our biannual remembrance service. The remembrance service is an evening event where people who have been recently bereaved gather together to share stories, laugh, cry, sing, and eat together. These events are well attended by whānau Māori, including tamariki.[5] Given this, I am exploring other ways to offer in-person connection between parents who are living *and* dying, and their children.

The reference list below reflects the reading that enabled the practice shared in this article. It is not intended to be exhaustive, or to represent the breadth of work that narrative practitioners have contributed to understanding death, dying, grief, loss or the use of narrative documentation. I look forward to utilising others' work and continuing to extend my practice. I have included further reading that highlights practitioners whose work has made significant contributions to narrative practices with people who are dying or experiencing grief.

Next steps: Accountability and collective practice?

I am the daughter of a parent whose mother died when he was 17, my childhood included a very unwell parent receiving cancer treatment, and I have faced my own child's mortality during a life-threatening illness. However, I do not have insider knowledge as a child whose parent died, or as a dying parent leaving children behind.

I hope to stay on the outside of this knowledge. I am aware of health privilege as I spend my workday supporting dying parents, then return home to the daily joys and chores of parenting. That I am a mother is a part of why Tūi chose me, and my mother-knowledges inform my work with dying parents. My accountability to Tūi, Theresa, Dani and others is to do my best to show up in my own mothering, and not take my privilege as a living mum for granted. I know that is what they would expect from me.

While children are at the centre of this project, I am not in relationship with the specific children, and I have only heard their responses to their letters second-hand. I have been led by their parents and trusted their discernment about what will and won't work for their children. I have offered to meet with children, and also to connect them with one another, as a way of broadening the horizon from individual to collective connection, and because young people may be more interested in connecting with one another than they are in connecting with me (Denborough, 2008). So far, the invitations have been declined. I will continue to extend invitations. However, I do not expect children to meet with me, and I am thinking of other ways I can express an ethic of accountability that do not impose on mourning children.

I am inspired by collective narrative practices that enable community and contribution (Denborough, 2008). I am currently taking steps towards meeting with adults I know, whose parents died when they were children. I am planning a meeting to invite their feedback. I am tentatively thinking about inviting adults with insider knowledge to be interviewed for or write letters to children whose parent has died, including their reflections on what they learnt from the experience, how they have got through hard times, and what their parent has contributed to their life. I love the idea of having a library of letters (again, inspired by leagues and archives) available for children whose parent is dying or has died (Denborough, 2018). However, that is jumping multiple steps ahead. First, I need to share, listen, learn and see what direction(s) the feedback of people with insider knowledge points me in. I look forward to continuing to learn and to becoming more useful for dying parents, and for their children.

Further reading

Enabling people to craft their own responses to grief
The crafting of grief: Constructing aesthetic responses to loss
by Lorraine Hedtke and John Winslade (2016)

Talking to children and families about death and grief
Death talk: Conversations with children and families by Glenda Fredman (1997)

Supporting families after the death of a child
"The politics of saying hullo again" by Helene Grau Kristensen (2021)

Narrative therapy in palliative care contexts
"Deciding how to die: Narrative therapy in palliative care with someone considering stopping dialysis" by Sasha Pilkington (2022)

Acknowledgments

Tūi, Theresa and Dani: Thank you for the invitation to support you and your families. You expanded my heart and showed me what the depth of mother-courage looks like. The gifts of your teaching have made me more useful for others. Thank you.

Theresa's and Dani's families: Thank you for your permission to share this work, and for the privilege of time shared together.

Te whānau ō North Haven Hospice Te Korowai Hūmarie: Ngā mihi nui ki a koutou. Thank you for the work we do together and for enabling me to stretch my practice to better support our communities.

Loretta: Thank you for your support and guidance across the one-year program, and for pointing me to Barbara Myerhoff when I worried that I was muddling maps.

Mark: Thank you for introducing me to narrative practice and for encouraging me to be brave.

To my children – for making me a mother. It is my best thing. I love you bigger than all the atoms.

Notes

[1] Please note: all names in this article are pseudonyms.

[2] Kia ora: "Hello (literal translation – be well) (to any number of people). Kia ora can mean hello, good morning, good afternoon and thank you" (Te Aka Māori Dictionary).

[3] Whānau: "Extended family, family group, a familiar term of address to a number of people - the primary economic unit of traditional Māori society. In the modern context the term is sometimes used to include friends who may not have any kinship ties to other members" (Te Aka Māori Dictionary).

[4] Pākehā: "New Zealander of European descent – probably applied to English-speaking Europeans living in Aotearoa/ New Zealand" (Te Aka Māori Dictionary).

[5] Tamariki: "Children – normally used only in the plural" (Te Aka Māori Dictionary).

References

Denborough, D. (2008). *Collective narrative practice.* Dulwich Centre Publications.

Denborough, D. (2018). *Do you want to hear a story? Adventures in collective narrative practice.* Dulwich Centre Publications.

Epston, D., & White, M. (1990). Consulting your consultants: The documentation of alternative knowledges. *Dulwich Centre Newsletter,* (4), 25–35.

Fredman, G. (1997). *Death talk: Conversations with children and families.* Routledge.

Hedtke, L., & Winslade, J. (2016). *The crafting of grief: Constructing aesthetic responses to loss.* Routledge.

Kristensen, H. G. (2021). The politics of saying hullo again. *Journal of Contemporary Narrative Therapy, 1,* 20–37.

Morgan, A. (2000). *What is narrative therapy? An easy-to-read introduction.* Dulwich Centre Publications.

Morgan, A. (2006). The position of the therapist in working with children. In M. White & A. Morgan (Eds.), *Narrative therapy with children and their families* (57–84). Dulwich Centre Publications.

Myerhoff, B. (1982). History among the elderly: Performance, visibility and remembering. In J. Ruby (Ed.), A crack in the mirror: Reflexive perspectives in anthropology (pp. 99–117). University of Pennsylvania Press.

Newman, D. (2008). Rescuing the said from the saying of it: Living documentation in narrative therapy. *International Journal of Narrative Therapy and Community Work.* (3), 24–34.

Pilkington, S. (2022). Deciding how to die: Narrative therapy in palliative care with someone considering stopping dialysis. *Journal of Contemporary Narrative Therapy, 2,* 28–67.

Te Aka Māori Dictionary. (2025). *Te Aka Māori Dictionary.* https://maoridictionary.co.nz

Weingarten, K. (2010). Reasonable hope: Construct, clinical applications, and supports. *Family process, 49*(1), 5–25. https://doi.org/10.1111/j.1545-5300.2010.01305.x

White, M. (1988). Saying hullo again: The incorporation of the lost relationship in the resolution of grief. *Dulwich Centre Newsletter,* (Spring), 7–11.

White, M. (2007). *Maps of narrative practice.* Norton.

From isolation to connection:

Young people, narrative practice and canine care

by Jack T. C. Chiu and Sharon S. K. Leung

Jack T. C. Chiu has worked as social worker for the past 28 years specialising in youth work in Hong Kong. With extensive experience in project development, training and supervision, he has worked on various youth issues, including delinquency, social withdrawal and mental wellness. Since 2007, he has integrated narrative therapy into his practice. Now residing in the UK with his family, he remains committed to advocating for youth empowerment and wellbeing. livethemoment100@gmail.com

Sharon S. K. Leung, PhD, taught social work and led training courses on narrative therapy at Hong Kong Baptist University, where she also served as the Director of the Centre for Youth Research and Practice until August 2020. Her journey with narrative practice began in 2001 when she attended an inspiring workshop by Michael White in Hong Kong. She continued her studies at Dulwich Centre in Adelaide and at The University of Melbourne. Over the past two decades, Sharon has been dedicated to indigenising narrative practice within China and Hong Kong. She and her family now reside in the UK. sksharon.leung@gmail.com

Chiu, T. C., & Leung, S. K. (2025). From isolation to connection: Young people, narrative practice and canine care. *International Journal of Narrative Therapy and Community Work*, (2), 21–31. https://doi.org/10.4320/CSDH7752

Author pronouns: Jack: he/him; Sharon: she/her

Abstract

This paper presents a project combining narrative practices and human–canine interaction to support young people in Hong Kong who were socially withdrawn and not in education, employment or training (NEET). Such youth often face societal stigmatisation and isolation. The "We Can" project paired participants with traumatised rescue dogs, fostering mutual healing and reconnection with the young people's preferred identities and their wider community. The paper examines how cultural and familial pressures can contribute to feelings of inadequacy. Using narrative therapy, the project emphasised participants' knowledge, competences, values and resilience rather than deficiencies. Caring for resilient dogs enabled participants to externalise their challenges and construct hopeful, empowering narratives. A key story shared in the paper is the transformational journey of a participant, referred to as Tarzan, who found his purpose through caring for dogs. His experiences, along with those of others, inspired broader personal and social commitments, as participants rejected societal expectations in favour of authentic and meaningful lives. The project challenged stereotypes about youth isolation, promoting reintegration while affirming the humanity and agency of marginalised young people in Hong Kong.

Key words: social withdrawal; social isolation; NEET; unemployment; youth; young people; human–canine interaction; animal-assisted therapy; dogs; Hong Kong; documents; collective narrative practice; narrative therapy

Chiu, T. C., & Leung, S. K. (2025). From isolation to connection: Young people, narrative practice and canine care. *International Journal of Narrative Therapy and Community Work*, (2), 21–31. https://doi.org/10.4320/CSDH7752

Author pronouns: Jack: he/him; Sharon: she/her

Intentions for this paper

We have several intentions in writing this paper. First, we would like to honour and document the knowledge, skills, values and principles of living of young people who have struggled with social withdrawal. Second, we would like to make available the knowledge and lived experiences of these young people in a way that might contribute to others who share similar struggles. By doing so, we hope that issues of social withdrawal are made visible, and that this may lead to less loneliness and despair. Lastly, we would like to share with people who are interested in narrative practice how working with these young people has moved and inspired us as practitioners.

"We Can": A project for young people struggling with social withdrawal

The narrative project "We Can" was carried out with young people in Hong Kong aged between 15 and 21 who had experienced social withdrawal. These are referred to as "hidden youth" in Hong Kong terminology. This was a small part of the innovative Career and Life Adventure Planning (CLAP) project led by Professor Victor Wong of Hong Kong Baptist University and funded by the Hong Kong Jockey Club Charities Trust. Author Sharon Leung was a research consultant on this project. The CLAP project aimed to reconnect young people with meaningful engagement in learning, careers or preferred leisure activities. Over five years, this community-wide initiative engaged 122 secondary schools, 115 youth-services nongovernment organisations and 3700 employers.

The We Can project within the broader CLAP initiative was given a Chinese name meaning "joining with dog companions" (狗狗同行). It aimed to support young people who had been secluded at home for over three months, and who were not in education, employment or training (NEET), to develop skills and competence, agency and aspiration. We Can combined narrative practice and animal-assisted therapy. It was initiated and designed by author Jack Chiu and his colleagues at the Evangelical Lutheran Church Social Service in Hong Kong, where he was then project manager. A unique part of this project was the involvement of Debbie Ngai, an animal-assisted therapist, who introduced the idea of working with dogs from an animal rescue shelter.

Principles of narrative practice in this project

Narrative ideas guided this project. We took steps to create contexts of practice that were safe, respectful, non-pathologising and valued young people's lived experience and insider knowledge. We supported the development of multiple stories and multiple identities. We resisted totalising identity conclusions about social withdrawal, incompetence, failure, uselessness and worthlessness. Instead, we worked with the young people to identify stories of competency in order to make visible their skills, values, knowledges of living, hopes and dreams. We invited the young people to remember and reconnect with their love, patience and kindness through caring for shelter dogs who had also been through hard times. The young people were invited to reflect on the significance of human–canine relationships and the mutual contributions they made to each other's lives. We critically examined normative cultural discourses because we believe that social norms and expectations are significant in constructing young people's lives, identities and relationships.

The phenomenon of social withdrawal

Social withdrawal refers to the avoidance of social interactions with others that results from anxiety or fear anticipated in a social context (Malti & Perren, 2011). A sense of belonging is seen as a basic human need. People are expected to build social and emotional connections with others and be accepted as a member of social groups. When young people choose to live a life of social isolation, this is assumed to be abnormal and raises mental health concerns from parents and professionals.

In human history, social isolation has not in all instances been seen as problematic. Priests or Buddhist monks have sought voluntary solitude as a means of inspiration, connection with nature, self-reflection and spiritual growth. People in ancient China who left high office and retreated as hermits were highly regarded for this act of resistance to the political regime. Recent discourse about social withdrawal as a psychological phenomenon was initiated in Japan by psychiatrist Tamaki Saito, who described "hikikomori" as having a "culture-bound psychiatric syndrome" (Teo & Gaw, 2010, p. 444). Teo (2012) described hikikomori as "modern-day hermits" who confine themselves at home and avoid social relationships, causing significant social dysfunction. Such withdrawal is not restricted to Japan. The terms "status zero" or "NEET" were first used in the UK to represent young people not engaged in education, employment or training (Bynner & Parsons, 2002). This label emphasises economic inactivity and suggests that government interventions are required to help young people make a successful transition between study and work. Other labels such as "slacker", "twixter" and "adultolescent" have been used to describe young people who live with their parents and have not achieved independence (Staff, 2013). Language such as "hidden youth" or "non-engaged youth" is frequently used in Hong Kong research (Li & Wong, 2015; Wong, 2012). Recently, "lying flat" (躺平) or "lying like a dead fish" (似一條死魚) have been used to describe young people who have given up struggling to meet expectations of success. These young people can be seen as seeking to free themselves from parental and school expectations and refusing to be exploited by neoliberalism.

According to data from the World Bank Group (2024), young people aged between 15 and 24 who have not engaged in education, employment or training for the previous six months are found in many countries, including Canada (11.7% of the total youth population in 2023), UK (12.8%), US (11.2%), Singapore (6.8%), India (23.5%), Australia (7.9%) and Hong Kong (5.9%). The label "NEET" carries negative connotations and may affect how young people perceive themselves. The World Bank data emphasises economic and human resources development and so provides limited utility in understanding the NEET phenomenon. We believe that the data does not represent the full range of experiences of these young people. Nor do mainstream discourses of social withdrawal that link it to mental health problems such as substance use, anxiety disorder, depression and self-harm (Gariépy et al., 2022). Social withdrawal is linked to school bullying, dysfunctional family interaction and fear of expectations and failure (Teo & Gaw, 2010). It is listed as an indicator for anxiety and depressive disorders (Li & Wong, 2015). Medical developmental psychopathology attributes social withdrawal to factors such as "aberrant brain processes, psychiatric conditions, unfavorable temperament, adverse family processes and excessive internet and media use" (Muris & Ollendick, 2023, p. 459). These dominant discourses draw attention to individual deficits and medical-psychological interventions, and give little attention to the effects of sociopolitical injustice on young people's lives.

Social withdrawal in Hong Kong

In Hong Kong, young people face intense pressure to succeed academically. This is underpinned by the belief that educational achievement secures wealth and career advancement. The cultural ideal that "a book holds a house of gold" drives families to invest heavily in their children's education. This often results in significant stress for both parents and students. Those who withdraw from school or work, sometimes turning to online gaming, are typically met with societal disapproval rather than empathy. Their disengagement is frequently interpreted as personal failure, and they may internalise labels such as "invisible" or "loser". These self-perceptions often stem from experiences of bullying, academic pressure and fear of disappointing family expectations. For many, withdrawal becomes a form of self-protection in the face of emotional strain and perceived injustice. Some express a desire not for success but for fairness, autonomy and relief from relentless pressure.

Social withdrawal among youth in Asian contexts, including China, is shaped by intersecting forces of gender, class and cultural norms. Girls are often expected to be obedient and family-oriented and may withdraw as a quiet form of resistance (Cheng & Furnham, 2004). Boys are pressured to embody academic and economic success, and failure to meet these ideals can lead to distress and disengagement. In this light, withdrawal may be seen as challenging dominant ideals of gender and achievement.

Disabled and neurodivergent individuals may withdraw, not because of inherent deficits but in response to social exclusion, sensory overwhelm, lack of accommodations or societal prejudice. Dominant narratives continue to pathologise neurodivergent ways of being, rather than recognising diverse forms of communication and participation.

Economic disadvantage further restricts access to education, leisure and peer networks, positioning withdrawal as a coping strategy amid structural inequality (Roberts, 2018). In capitalist societies like Hong Kong, withdrawal is often stigmatised as a moral or personal shortcoming, deepening the shame experienced by those who disengage.

Narrative practice offers a powerful framework for understanding youth withdrawal not as a personal failing but as a form of resistance. White (2002, p. 46) argued that such refusals can be seen as signs of the "partial failure" of modern power – the power that encourages individuals to shape their identities and lives according to socially constructed norms. From this perspective, withdrawal can be seen as a meaningful act that disrupts dominant scripts of success and conformity. Narrative practices can help young people to explore the significance of their actions, make sense of their resistance, and re-author alternative stories about their lives, values and relationships.

Project outline

The young people who participated in this project were referred by parents, social workers or practitioners from local schools and youth organisations. Many of these young people exhibited fear of social interaction, having remained at home in isolation for months or even years. During home visits conducted by the project team, we were careful to avoid intruding on the lives of the young people, instead prioritising respect for their autonomy and preferences. Establishing a sense of safety and trust was essential, and team members refrained from initiating direct conversations with the young people until such trust had been developed. Instead, initial interactions often involved engaging with parents and other family members. Although families were often eager to facilitate communication between the team and the youth, team members emphasised the importance of respecting the young people's choices and pace of engagement. In their interactions with families, team members focused on identifying the young person's interests. Notably, they learnt that many had a history of caring for pets including cats, dogs, rabbits, tortoises and hamsters. While the young people avoided discussing personal matters or engaging in social interactions with other humans, they showed kindness and affection towards the animals they cared for. This observation highlighted a unique aspect of their emotional expression and capacity for connection, even in the context of significant social withdrawal. As we began to learn about their experiences of quitting school, the young people reported bullying, rejection and anxiety about academic demands. However, when describing their relationships with their pets, they expressed a sense of security and happiness, and a longing for genuine and nonjudgemental connections.

We invited the young people to consider visiting and offering help to shelter dogs. Team members shared stories of the dogs with the young people, describing how the dogs had been abused, traumatised and abandoned by their previous carers and ended up in the shelter. The young people were invited to reflect on any resonances with their own experiences.

Those who chose to join the program were given training on how to examine the physical health and emotional condition of the dogs. During their initial visits to the shelter, they noticed that these traumatised dogs were timid, anxious and often indifferent to human contact. The dogs were in poor health and in a poor living environment. Training was provided on how to approach, care for and support dogs emotionally. Animal welfare was a core element. The young people's observations about the dogs, the care they provided and the meaning of their volunteer work were reflected on in small groups and carefully documented.

After a few visits, the young people noticed that dogs under their care had become calmer and more relaxed. They expressed satisfaction because the human–canine relationship offered comforting companionship to them both. Their interest in animal care and welfare were linked to other animal-related fields of work such as hotels for dogs, animal food or product sales, animal grooming and ecological tourism. Through caring for the dogs, the young people started to communicate with others volunteering at the shelter. Some became assistant trainers in the shelter, helping to coach other new volunteers to care for the dogs.

Integrating narrative practice and animal-assisted therapy

Traditional animal-assisted therapy emphasises the healing power of service and therapy dogs on distressed humans. The We Can project, in contrast, emphasised mutual support and healing of both the young people and the traumatised dogs. The project aimed to provide young people with a way to reconnect with themselves, others and the world around them through building relationships with and supporting the shelter dogs in combination with using narrative practices to support meaning-making about this experience.

The human–canine interaction required little spoken expression and human interaction, so it facilitated the young people's participation without causing too much anxiety and discomfort. Dogs are nonjudgemental, offer unconditional acceptance and respond to genuine care. These relationship qualities provided a nonthreatening context in which the young people could demonstrate their ability to establish connections and receive validation in ways often lacking in their human relationships.

The human–canine interactions provided multiple openings for team members to invite the young people to tell their stories in the context of resonance with the dogs' experiences of abandonment, survival and trust-building. Through learning to recognise the dogs' survival strategies, the young people were supported to externalise their struggles and talk about their own challenges more freely. This created opportunities to develop a shared narrative about overcoming adversity, and to reconsider negative identity conclusions like "lazy", "wasting life" and "internet-addicted" in light of skills and knowledge developed when facing adversity.

Co-construction of human–canine relationships and identities

The young people were invited to reflect on why they enjoyed being with the dogs, what they and the dogs could offer to each other, and how such contributions were made possible. They also thought about the meaning of care, their hopes and dreams for the dogs, and the possible future they could co-create through the relationship. The young people expressed gratitude for the dogs' genuine trust, acceptance, kindness, lack of judgement and companionship. They recognised their own contributions to the relationship, particularly through providing care, love, respect, play and protection, as well as a clean living place and sometimes a better chance of being adopted in the future. They witnessed changes in the dogs, from being timid and withdrawn to trusting and accepting their care, and then to leaving their cages to explore and play.

The young people witnessed how the traumatised dogs were resilient and responsive to their love and care, despite adversity, abandonment and a poor shelter environment. The dogs' reactions inspired the young people to overcome personal difficulties such as physical discomfort, anxiety and fear of communication. Through re-membering practices (White, 2007), the young people discovered their knowledge of kindness, skills of care and purpose in life through rich description and reconnection with their lived experiences, including other significant relationships with pets and people. This discovery not only gave them a sense of comfort, confidence and love but also encouraged them to spend more time with significant people around them and remain hopeful in relationships and the future.

Some young people expressed a preference for interacting with dogs rather than people. We explored this through a focus on the values that might be "absent but implicit" in this preference (White, 2011). In this light, withdrawal from human connection could be seen not simply as avoidance, but also as an expression of preferences about relationships. This focus allowed the team to honour the young people's relational preferences and their particular ethics of care. Their bond with the dogs was an opening to conversations about the kinds of human relationships they valued – ones built on respect, equality, kindness, compassion, nonjudgement, acceptance and mutual care. The human–canine relationship offered a safe space where these values could be experienced and affirmed, helping to clarify what meaningful connection looked and felt like for them.

The young people in this project displayed significant compassion for the dogs. Through the understanding they gained of the pet industry and its operations, they became keen to advocate for animals' rights. They spoke up about abandoning pets, treating animals with cruelty and practices of commodification. They advocated for adoption, particularly for aged dogs. Some explored the possibility of becoming foster carers for animals. They changed on a personal level, to be more genuine, kind and relaxed, and on a political level, to want to change the destiny of dogs, advocating for animals' rights and wellbeing, and respecting and treasuring life and relationships in general. Apart from searching for their preferred lifestyle, they also challenged the dominant ideology of modern life, with its fast-paced money-status-material-achievement orientation.

The following paragraphs share the journey of one of the participants, a young person nicknamed Tarzan. A medical social worker gave Tarzan this nickname because he had long hair, which reminded the social worker of the fictional character who was raised by apes in the jungle (Burroughs, 1912). When we sought Tarzan's consent to share his story in this paper, we asked him about the name he preferred to use. He agreed to use Tarzan because he said he would like to be thought of as an animal lover and protector of nature. Jack did not record all his conversations with Tarzan, but he did write down many of Tarzan's thoughts about the purposes of life, and the values and commitments that were important to him.

Tarzan's story

Tarzan, a 17-year-old referred by his medical social worker, had been isolated at home for over two years.

His mother was concerned about his insomnia, lack of communication and constant internet use, suspecting addiction or mental health issues. The family criticised him for dropping out of school and spending time on comics and games.

At our first meeting, Tarzan was reluctant to speak. I (Jack) noticed he was holding a comic book featuring animals and used this as an entry point for conversation. I asked if he liked animals and introduced the idea of volunteering at a dog shelter. Volunteering at the shelter – feeding and caring for dogs – requires minimal verbal interaction and I wondered if it might help Tarzan to reconnect gradually with others. When I invited him to join, he didn't commit immediately.

Warm up exercise: Animal-related stories as a collective theme

On the first day of the volunteer service, eight young people who had been in social isolation for different durations participated, including Tarzan. We met Debbie, an animal-assisted therapist who trains volunteers and uses animals in therapy to support emotional and social wellbeing. Debbie shared the basic rules and information that the volunteers needed to know about dog care. I asked the young people to choose an animal to represent themselves and to write down ways in which they were similar to this animal. I also prepared an exercise using a collective narrative timeline. Denborough (2008, p. 144) described this practice as "a method that enabled participants to share powerful personal memory and history but in a way that linked to a collective theme. It brought people together while also acknowledging a great diversity of experience". I hoped that producing a collective timeline would be a useful way to help the participants feel comfortable in this first meeting, and it powerfully honoured the knowledge of everyone in the room. The group drew a timeline on a long piece of paper on the floor of the activity room. This was divided into ages and their corresponding school grades. I invited the group to reflect on their experiences with:

- any animal

- knowledge and stories of caring for animals

- an intention, a wish, a learning or a value that is important to them and their relationship with animals.

To make the participants feel comfortable, I invited each person to think about the following (drawing on Denborough, 2008):

- What is the history of this intention/wish/ commitment/hope/learning or value and when did it begin?

- How old were you or what grade were you in?

- Where did you learn this?

- Who did you learn it from?

Because they were not used to talking or socialising, we provided each participant with sticky notes and animal cards we designed to help them express their thoughts, either in simple words or drawings. Then, they were invited to stick their pieces of paper on the timeline at the appropriate year/age. After doing this, they walked around the timeline and read each other's notes. They were also invited to ask questions about other stories or drawings on this collective timeline. For most, this was their first time engaging in a group activity in some time, so they chose to write on the sticky notes and select animal cards to place on the collective timeline but declined to ask questions.

Tarzan chose a picture of an owl to represent him. He placed a sticky note on the picture saying "silence, observation, avoid people and noise, show up in the dark".

Matching young people with rescued dogs

Debbie briefed the participants about why the dogs needed their care, which was to help the dogs reconnect with and trust humans so they could have a better chance of being adopted. Debbie had screened the dogs in advance to identify those that she considered safe. She introduced each dog to the participants, describing its temperament. Then, they were invited to choose a dog they wanted to serve. To create an opening to their personal stories, I invited each young person to consider the knowledge, skills, values or commitments that informed their choice of dog.

Tarzan chose a dog that was described as timid, sensitive and insecure. He mumbled a few words about the values and skills he could bring to caring for this particular dog, which included patience, observation and kindness.

Resonance with the dog's adverse experience

After the first two visits to the dog shelter, Tarzan appeared upset and asked a question for the very first time. His dog was unwilling to try the food he had prepared. He asked Debbie if this was his fault.

This presented an opportunity to invite Debbie to talk about why the dogs were so timid, and the state they had been in when they were found. Debbie said that the dogs had been skinny and malnourished, with skin infections. They had been found in isolated environments where they could hide from threats and dangers.

The young people listened attentively and showed sympathy for the dogs. I then invited them to think about the following questions in relation to their own experience to encourage understanding and connection with the dogs:

- What do you think the dogs have experienced?

- Why do you think the dogs display this current behaviour?

- Is there any resonance with your own stories of challenge?

- Can you share ways you have responded to or resisted adversities?

- Are your experiences of adversity and despair okay, not okay, or a bit of both?

- If you could name the problem you have been dealing with, what name would you give it?

Here are some of the wisdoms Tarzan identified in the experiences of the dogs:

Dogs can … ignore the noise, stay calm.

Observe, be patient, stay away from harm.

Do things they feel comfortable with.

I asked Tarzan, "What makes you think the dogs are doing these things?" and "Do these qualities resonate with your own skills of resistance to problems?" He replied:

I can feel how the dogs feel. These dogs were probably unable to do things their owner wanted and were abandoned … People expect others to do the things they want you to do.

Sometimes I wonder why I have to put effort into something other people regard as useful or important and give up something I feel is interesting.

I can ignore other's "noise" like the dogs do.

Tarzan pointed out that it was people's "noise" (judgements and demands) that caused him distress,

leading him to isolate himself. As Tarzan and the other young people progressed through the program and learnt more about the suffering of the dogs, their silent participation was replaced with expressions of empathy and connection.

Skills and knowledge about surviving difficult times

We designed a volunteer journal (狗狗同行手冊) to record the young people's observations of the dogs and of their own knowledge and skills in facing adversity. The participants documented the strategies the dogs used to overcome challenges and connected these insights with their own experiences of similar themes or concerns. They were then invited to record their personal knowledge and skills. Such "documents of knowledge" (Fox, 2003) can be invaluable for individuals at risk of losing sight of their preferred identities, helping them regain a sense of agency and control in their lives.

Tarzan used his volunteer journal to document his observations about how the dogs had been able to survive tough times:

Dogs live simple and direct lives. They have no complicated thoughts.

Dogs try hard to survive and stay away from harm.

They are seldom bothered by the environment, even though the shelter is noisy and in poor condition.

He documented what he had been doing in response to the hard times he faced, including how he survived the "noise" that bothered him:

Play songs, just don't care about people's comments.

Keep noise away. Wear earphones, even without music on.

Do something else. Play video games.

Caring about things (and dogs). I care. Focusing on how I can do better.

Watching documentaries like Animal Planet is healing.

Stay silent, listen and observe.

In these journal entries, Tarzan recorded how he had been actively resisting oppression from noise. This provided him with a sense of agency and a sense of himself as the author of his own life.

Caring for traumatised dogs provided opportunities for the young people to reflect on their life challenges in new ways. Tarzan shared how he stayed calm and observant despite the noise. He told us how he had learnt to protect himself from difficult life situations. Tarzan's sharing reminded me of what Michael White once wrote:

> No-one is a passive recipient of trauma. People always take steps in endeavouring to prevent the trauma they are subject to, and, when preventing this trauma is clearly impossible, they take steps to try to modify it in some way or modify its effects on their lives. (White, 2006, p. 28)

Double-storied accounts about treasured values

White (2000) described double listening as hearing both the hardship and the person's response to it, including what is "absent but implicit". Participants shared challenges they faced, such as staying silent, withdrawing at home, and turning to the internet or games – strategies that were often misunderstood or dismissed by their families. For many, this group was the first space where their coping methods were acknowledged and respected as valid efforts towards self-preservation and wellbeing. Gradually, they grew more confident in sharing their stories.

After reading about Tarzan's strategies for staying away from noise, I asked:

Jack: If the noise makes you want to stay away from others, what does that say about what's important to you in relationships?

Tarzan: It means people shouldn't press others to follow their pace and do what they believe to be important.

Jack: So, would you like to share what is important to you?

Tarzan: Paying attention to detail, trying my best to prepare food for the dogs. These are things people around me despise but I believe it to be important.

This reflection shifted our conversation from problem-saturated talk towards naming what mattered most to him: respect for choice and individual differences.

Tarzan spoke about the distress caused by noise, which he described as insincere concern and rigid expectations from adults:

> Some people want me to act how they expect. It's not genuine care. Even in the family, they say they want you to be happy, but only if you do what they want. I stay silent and away. I do my best to protect myself.

Tarzan's retreat wasn't passive: it was an intentional strategy to shield himself from judgement and maintain emotional integrity.

From personal issues to injustice and oppression in the social context

After listening to Tarzan's account of the problems related to noise, I was interested to know whether he felt okay, not okay or a bit of both about the effects caused by the noise and why. He replied:

> People categorise others according to their performance. They focus on what the majority regard as good and ignore those who don't fit in. When you do not conform to their standards, you will lose everyone's respect. Just like you are living in profound loneliness.

> Some dogs are active and outgoing while others are slow and introverted. Every dog has its own pace. Why can't I have my own pace? Their timetable is not mine.

Tarzan expressed disagreement with societal expectations and standards. He had his own values, which involved respecting individual pace and choice.

A wonderful moment in the dog shelter

After a few sessions of human–canine interaction, the trust and bond between dogs and the young volunteers had developed significantly. We believed that it would be worthwhile to acknowledge this development, so we asked the young people about their experiences of caring for the dogs. Most importantly, we invited them to share their perceptions of the dogs' experience of their service to them. We asked, in the eyes of the dog you are caring for:

- What personal qualities are they admiring/loving about you?

- What challenges have you overcome during the service?

- What knowledge and skills have you used to help improve your relationship with the dogs?

- What values, commitments or hopes have you been holding on to in your caring work with dogs?

In narrative practice, documentation of positive identity conclusions is used to help people whose sense of identity is at risk (White, 1995). We invited the young people to share and write down their new discoveries at the end of each dog caring session. Tarzan's reflections in his journal included the following:

> Dog validated my existence! Never feel so welcomed by anybody.
>
> Dogs react positively to people who treat them well and stay away from those who are not good to them. Dogs do not judge. They are straightforward. They do not care whether you are good or bad looking, smart or dumb, normal or abnormal. They care about someone who really treats them well.
>
> Dogs knew my wholehearted contribution to them.
>
> They let me know I am important. What I have tried hard with or contributed to is worthwhile. Somebody will know it. I would keep going with what I believe to be worthwhile.

Through this journaling in response to the questions above, Tarzan reconnected with neglected aspects of his lived experience. Acknowledgments and validation of self from the dogs and others had become available to Tarzan. This allowed him to author a new, preferred story of his life.

Conclusion

This work explored how dogs might "participate" in narrative practice. Rather than serving as a therapeutic tool, the dogs emerged as a significant presence – a kind of person – whose attunement and responses created space for the young people to feel seen, heard and valued in ways that unsettled dominant narratives of failure or deviance. Through these interspecies encounters, young people experienced moments of recognition that traditional human-centred practices had often failed to offer. In this light, the dogs' role was not ancillary but ethically and relationally central, challenging us to reconsider the boundaries of meaning-making and the agents who participate in it. This reorientation invited further attention to how interspecies relationality can disrupt grand narratives

and make visible the dignity, labour and humanity of those often marginalised in therapeutic and social spaces.

The social workers and narrative practitioners involved in this project spoke powerfully about how their relationships with young people were not only transformative for the youth, but also deeply reshaped their own lives. Rather than stepping into roles of authority, the practitioners saw themselves as collaborators. This collaboration was grounded in mutual learning, respect and care. Inspired by Michael White's "taking-it-back practice" (1997), practitioners reflected on how the insights, creativity and resistance of the young people influenced both their professional commitments and personal growth. Many described being reconnected with the core values that first called them to this work – rediscovering courage, humility and a renewed sense of purpose. Stepping beyond comfort zones, the practitioners stood side by side with young people in the shared care of shelter dogs. This became an act of solidarity, not charity: a shared ethical stance, as Vikki Reynolds described it, "the connective practice of resisting oppression and promoting justice-doing" (2019, p. 9).

This collaboration between practitioners, young people and rescued animals became a living expression of collective care, in which power was shared and voices were honoured. The often-unheard stories of both young people and dogs were not only acknowledged but valued as forms of resistance and dignity.

As practitioners, we remain accountable, not as experts but as companions in struggle, challenging structural injustice and nurturing spaces where hope can take root. The young people reminded us that even within systems that attempt to silence and marginalise, there is still room to reclaim identity, dignity and possibility. The young people's transformations deepened our own collective belief that life is not only survivable, but beautiful and full of potential when we walk together in solidarity.

Acknowledgments

We would like to express our sincere gratitude to Tarzan and the other participants in the We Can project. Special thanks to the dedicated social work practitioners, Debbie Ngai and the dog shelter manager. Additionally, we extend our appreciation to Professor Victor Wong of HKBU, ELCHK, and the Hong Kong Jockey Club Charity for their contributions.

References

Barzeva, S. A., Meeus, W. H. J., & Oldehinkel, A. J. (2019). Social withdrawal in adolescence and early adulthood: Measurement issues, normative development, and distinct trajectories. *Journal of Abnormal Child Psychology, 47(*5), 865–879. https://doi.org/10.1007/s10802-018-0497-4

Burroughs, E. R. (1912). *Tarzan of the apes.* McClurg.

Bynner, J., & Parsons, S. (2002). Social exclusion and the transition from school to work: The case of young people not in education, employment, or training (NEET). *Journal of Vocational Behavior, 60*(2), 289–309. https://doi.org/10.1006/jvbe.2001.1868

Cheng, S. T., & Furnham, A. (2004). Personality, peer relations, and family factors as predictors of social withdrawal in Chinese adolescents. *Journal of Adolescence, 27*(3), 299–312. https://doi.org/10.1006/jado.2002.0475

Denborough, D. (2008). *Collective narrative practice: Responding to individuals, groups and communities who have experienced trauma.* Dulwich Centre Publications.

Fox, H. (2003). Using therapeutic documents: a review. *International Journal of Narrative Therapy and Community Work, (4).* 25–35.

Gariépy, G., Danna, S. M., Hawke, L., Henderson, J., & Iyer, S. N. (2022). The mental health of young people who are not in education, employment, or training: A systematic review and meta-analysis. *Social Psychiatry and Psychiatric Epidemiology, 57,* 1107–1121. https://doi.org/10.1007/s00127-021-02212-8

Li, T. M. H., & Wong, P. W. C. (2015). Youth social withdrawal behavior (hikikomori): A systematic review of qualitative and quantitative studies. *Australian and New Zealand Journal of Psychiatry, 49,* 595–609. https://doi.org/10.1177/0004867415581179

Malti, T., & Perren, S. (2011). Social competence. In B. B. Brown & M. J. Prinstein (Eds.), *Encyclopedia of adolescence* (pp. 332–340). Springer.

Muris, P., & Ollendick, T. H. (2023). Contemporary hermits: A developmental psychopathology account of extreme social withdrawal (hikikomori) in young people. *Clinical Child and Family Psychology Review, 26,* 459–481. https://doi.org/10.1007/s10567-023-00425-8

Reynolds, V. (2019). *Justice-doing at the intersections of power.* Dulwich Centre Publications.

Roberts, S. (2018). Young working-class men's experiences of marginalisation and resistance. *Journal of Youth Studies, 21*(5), 597–613. https://doi.org/10.1080/13676261.2017.1394990

Staff, J. (2013). Coming of age in America: The transition to adulthood in the twenty-first century. *Contemporary Sociology: A Journal of Review, 42*(1), 117–118. https://doi.org/10.1177/0093061112468721hh

Teo, A. R. (2012, November 30). *Modern-day hermits: The story of hikikomori in Japan and beyond* [YouTube video]. University of Michigan Centre for Japanese Studies. https://www.youtube.com/watch?v=70bv5gaN4LI

Teo, A. R., & Gaw, A. C. (2010). Hikikomori, a Japanese culture-bound syndrome of social withdrawal? A proposal for DSM-V. *Journal of Nervous and Mental Disease, 198*(6), 444–449. https://doi.org/10.1097/NMD.0b013e3181e086b1

White, M. (1995). Reflecting teamwork as definitional ceremony. In M. White, *Re-authoring lives: Interviews and essays* (pp. 172–198). Dulwich Centre Publications.

White, M. (1997). *Narratives of therapists' lives.* Dulwich Centre Publications.

White, M. (2000). Re-engaging with history: The absent but implicit. In M. White, *Reflections on narrative practice: Essays and interviews* (pp. 35–58). Dulwich Centre Publications.

White, M. (2002). Addressing personal failure. *International Journal of Narrative Therapy and Community Work, (3),* 33–76.

White, M. (2006). Working with people who are suffering the consequences of multiple trauma: A narrative perspective. In D. Denborough (Ed.), *Trauma: Narrative responses to traumatic experience* (pp. 25–85). Dulwich Centre Publications.

White, M. (2007). *Maps of narrative practice.* Norton.

White, M. (2011). Revaluation and resonance: Narrative responses to traumatic experience. In D. Denborough (Ed.), *Narrative practice: Continuing the conversations* (pp. 123–133). Norton.

Wong, V. (2012). Social withdrawal as invisible youth disengagement: Government inaction and NGO responses in Hong Kong. *International Journal of Sociology and Social Policy, 32*(7/8), 415–430. https://doi.org/10.1108/01443331211249057

World Bank Group. (2024). *Unemployment, youth total (% of total labor force ages 15-24) (modeled ILO estimate).* https://data.worldbank.org/indicator/SL.UEM.1524.ZS

Psychedelic-assisted therapy from a narrative therapy perspective:

A map for practitioners

by Christine Dennstedt

Christine Dennstedt has been active in Vancouver's narrative therapy community since completing her master's degree in 2002. Over the next decade, she trained, practiced, published and developed innovative narrative group practices at Peak House, a residential substance-use program. She earned her PhD in 2010 through the TAOS Institute under Dr Sheila McNamee with research on the intersections of substance misuse and disordered eating among young women. Now based in Whistler, Christine maintains a private practice and contributes to emerging developments linking psychedelic medicines, mental health and narrative therapy. @insider.knowledges christinedennstedt@gmail.com

ORCID ID: https://orcid.org/0009-0001-0009-9405

Abstract

Psychedelic-assisted therapy is currently in its second wave and enjoying a renaissance of sorts. This article describes a narrative therapy–inspired approach to working therapeutically with psychedelics. My intent in writing this paper is to provide a model for how narrative therapy ideas in practice can be applied to the three stages of psychedelic-assisted therapy: preparation, medicine work and integration. In describing this map for practitioners, the rites of passage metaphor, as applied therapeutically by Michael White, is used to outline the phases a person will move through in their psychedelic-assisted therapy journey.

Key words: psychedelic; psilocybin; ketamine; rites of passage; migration of identity; narrative practice; narrative therapy

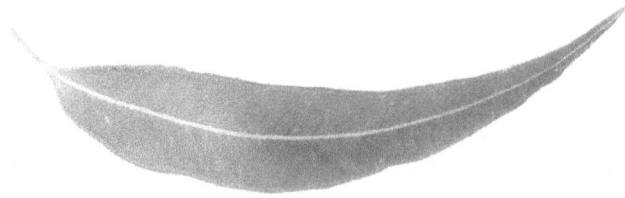

Dennstedt, C. (2025). Psychedelic-assisted therapy from a narrative therapy perspective: A map for practitioners. *International Journal of Narrative Therapy and Community Work*, (2), 32–48. https://doi.org/10.4320/NGOQ2236

Author pronouns: she/her

This paper describes a narrative therapy–informed (White & Epston, 1990) approach to psychedelic-aided therapy.[1] My hope is to offer additional practices from narrative therapy to people already working therapeutically with psychedelics in contexts where this is legally permitted, noting that legality varies by substance and regulatory pathway.

Rather than seeing problems as representative of an inherent flaw or disease within a person, narrative therapists view problems as being separate from the person's identity. This orientation creates space for the person to see their experience from a different perspective, in ways that allow for a new unfolding of meaning to occur and new preferred stories to be told. In this paper, I describe ways in which I have sought to create a form of psychedelic-assisted therapy that draws on narrative therapy to help create and strengthen a person's new and preferred story.

Safety and agency

In my therapeutic practice, I am aware of both the potential benefits and the potential risks psychedelics pose, both for persons being treated and also for practitioners (Fadiman, 2011). Thorough screening processes are thus necessary to safeguard against potential harm when working in this area, and it is of utmost importance to note that psychedelic therapy is not suitable for all persons. Exclusion criteria for psychedelic-assisted therapy can be related to physical health, psychiatric health, medication use, or any combination of these (Carhart-Harris et al., 2021; Griffiths et al., 2016).

Ethical considerations are critical, given the potency of psychedelics and their ability to induce profound psychological and emotional experiences. Practitioners need to conscientiously assess safety factors for persons entering therapy in which psychedelics are used. Particularly if persons have had experiences of trauma, sexualised violence or gender-based violence, it is necessary that there be conversations about safety, gender and power relations to safeguard the person's wellbeing and agency. Should a person be concerned that they might encounter something or someone that has injured them in any way, we can ask how we can support them if this occurs during the psychedelic journey, how they can let us know that they need support, and what they might want to be reminded of or told if this occurs. Therapists working with psychedelics need to be committed

to ensuring and prioritising the safety of the persons who consult them. In light of recent and deeply concerning allegations of sexual harm involving therapists using psychedelic-assisted practices (Multidisciplinary Association for Psychedelic Studies [MAPS], 2019, 2021b), it is strongly recommended that practitioners work in co-therapy teams – often composed of one male and one female therapist – rather than in isolation. This team-based approach helps foster a safer therapeutic environment for both the person engaging in the psychedelic-assisted therapy and the therapists themselves (Johnson et al., 2008; MAPS, 2021a). One of our primary responsibilities in a narrative therapy–informed approach to psychedelic-assisted therapy is to co-create and sustain a territory of safety, a space where people can meaningfully explore new knowledges and re-memberings, and begin to weave these into the ongoing re-authoring of their lives.

Cultural accountability

Psychedelic plants and fungi have been used by Indigenous peoples and cultures for healing and spiritual purposes for millennia (Carod-Artal, 2015; Pollan, 2018). These can be part of sacramental practices involving rites of passage, rituals and ceremony. There is evidence that psychedelics have shaped certain cultures and religions dating back to 5000 BCE (Samorini, 2019).

The use of psilocybin, a psychedelic compound found in certain mushrooms, has its roots in Indigenous healing practices, particularly among Mazatec communities in Mexico, who have used it ceremonially for centuries. I say this to honour the importance of engaging in this work in ethically accountable ways – approaching it with integrity, humility and a commitment to avoiding cultural appropriation. The success and therapeutic potential of these medicines cannot be separated from the wisdom traditions that have carried them. My practice includes naming the origins of these medicines when speaking with clients, staying informed about the historical and cultural contexts from which the medicines come, supporting Indigenous-led organisations and advocacy, and not to extracting or replicating ceremonial elements outside their original context (Richards, 2017). Accountability also means continuing to reflect on my own positionality and remaining open to critique, unlearning and dialogue.

In Indigenous communities, there is concern about the many ways that traditional medicines are being culturally appropriated by Western medicine (Celidwen, 2022).

> The resurgence of the Western psychedelic movement has ... led to increasing concerns from many Indigenous Nations regarding the cultural appropriation of their traditional medicines, a lack of recognition of the sacred positioning of these medicines within their communities and cultures, exclusionary practices in research and scale up endeavours, and the threat to their intellectual property rights with patents of traditional Indigenous medicines. (Celidwen et al., 2022, p .1)

In 1957, "Seeking the Magic Mushroom", a photo essay by Gordon Wasson, was published in *Life* magazine (Wasson, 1957). It documented a psilocybin journey guided by Mazatec curandera Maria Sabina. Following this publication, many Americans headed to Mexico in search of the "magic mushroom". Gordon Wasson betrayed Maria Sabina both by publishing the photos of his psilocybin journey and by not keeping her identity secret as he had promised. As a result, Maria Sabina was briefly jailed and her house was set on fire (Siff, 2018). Soon after the publication, a compound in psilocybin was isolated and the process to do so patented by Sandoz pharmaceuticals (Gerber et al., 2021). "From an indigenous perspective, psilocybin research and drug development tell a story of extraction, cultural appropriation, bioprospecting, and colonization" (Gerber et al., 2021, p. 574). Furthermore, some plant medicines such as peyote cactus (from which the psychedelic mescaline is derived, and which is central to the religious practices of the Native American Church) are at risk of extinction. This is linked to detrimental land use including over-harvesting and improper harvesting techniques, psychedelic tourism, and land development causing loss of habitat for the sacred cactus (Pollan, 2021).

A narrative map to guide us when working therapeutically with psychedelics

I have adapted this map from Michael White's (1997) practice with "migrations of identity", as developed with persons separating from addiction. White drew on rites of passage theory as described by van Gennep (1960) and Turner (1969), who identified three stages: separation, transition and incorporation. White reworked these concepts into a therapeutic map that highlights the significance of meaningful life transitions. Turner's notion of ritual and the liminal "realm of possibility" (1969) also inform the map I present here, though it is White's application that gives these ideas a distinct therapeutic utility and relevance within narrative practice.

Psychedelic-assisted therapy typically has three distinct phases: preparation sessions, medicine session(s) and integration sessions (Fadiman, 2011; Mithoefer, 2017).[2] These three phases of psychedelic-assisted therapy fit well and are congruent with White's (1997) rites of passage metaphor. White described the rites of passage phases as follows:

> First is the *separation phase*, at which a person breaks from their life as they know it. This marks the beginning of their journey. Second, there is the *liminal phase*. This is a "betwixt and between" phase, in which one's familiar sense of being in the world is absent ... Third, this is the *reincorporation phase* [which] is achieved when a person finds that they've arrived at another place in life ... At this time, persons regain a sense of being knowledgeable and skilled in matters of living. (White, 1997, p. 4)

Rites of passage metaphor

A rites of passage metaphor that includes separation, transition/liminality and reincorporation/integration acts as a guide to the territories the person will be exploring during their psychedelic-assisted therapeutic journey. When working with people who will be entering extra-ordinary states of consciousness, we need to be clear about the work that will be required of them in each phase to provide a sense of what lies ahead and what is expected. This can enable the person to adequately and confidently prepare for each phase of the journey. The rites of passage metaphor allow us to support persons as they imagine and prepare for the journey they will be embarking on, the possible thresholds they will be crossing, and potential stumbling blocks or setbacks they may encounter. We want to get a clear sense of what values, knowledges, skills or practices, and perhaps even people and other creatures, are important for them to metaphorically bring with them as supportive allies on their psychedelic-assisted therapy journey. We can also ask about anything they would like to leave behind.

Sometimes, people undertaking psychedelic-assisted therapy experience a shift in perspective that leads to alternative understandings, possibilities for movement, and/or reconnection with themselves or their community. Psychedelics transport some people to a place where they experience a sense of oneness with the universe, a sense of belonging and sacredness (Fadiman, 2011). When a person has a psychedelic experience involving such a sense of wonder, I have found that narrative therapy practices can assist in scaffolding questions about relational interconnectedness with plants, nature and other sentient beings, and can also generate movement away from a view of problems as individual experiences or disorders and towards recognition of their social and relational contexts, and the importance of healing within community.

I will briefly describe the phases that I have developed using a rites of passage metaphor to inform a narrative approach to psychedelic therapy and give examples of questions that can be used for each phase of the work.

1. Separation and preparation phase

Leaving the known and familiar: What are you separating from?
This part of the process invites reflection on what the person is beginning to seek distance from, whether that be problem-saturated stories or ways of being that no longer align with their values.

Setting intentions and moving towards what matters
Here, the focus turns to what the person is migrating towards: the hopes, values and preferred ways of living that carry vitality and meaning. Through intention setting and therapeutic conversation, space is made for clarity, direction and reorientation towards what matters most.

2. Transition/liminal phase: The psychedelic journey

Crossing the threshold
The medicine session marks an entry into the in-between – a threshold space where known identities loosen and new knowledges, stories and meanings may be experienced.

Betwixt and between: Liminality and early integration
In the hours and days following the medicine session, the person may continue to dwell in a liminal state. New images, emotions or realisations may begin to emerge, not yet fully formed but rich with possibility. This is a fertile time for reflection and gentle meaning-making: a bridge between the session and life beyond it.

3. Reincorporation/integration phase: Weaving new meaning into daily life

In this stage, persons work to integrate the values, intentions and knowledges that emerged or that they reconnected with during their experience, allowing them to shape daily life in preferred ways.

4. Hazards and comebacks

The last aspect of this journey involves potential hazards and comebacks as the person prepares for and moves through the phases of their therapeutic psychedelic journey.

I will weave in the voices of some of the persons who have consulted me to illustrate each phase described here. One person is a man whom I will call Fred (a pseudonym). Under Health Canada's Special Access Program (SAP), he was approved for psilocybin-assisted psychotherapy to address long-standing struggles with depression, including a diagnosis of treatment-resistant depression.[3] Fred had been prescribed multiple antidepressants, electroconvulsive shock therapy (ECT) and talk therapy, all to no avail, and had lived with what he called the "crushing weight" of depression for over 20 years. When we first met, he spoke about the powerful grip that depression had on him and shared some of the deeply held beliefs he had been living with. For example, he described feeling at times that he was "too stupid to live", "fatally flawed", and that he "had a personality disorder". He said he was "a liability to loved ones", "a black hole" and "not able to work".

Separation and preparation

Leaving the known and familiar: What are you separating from?

When persons are coming to us for psychedelic-assisted therapy, they are clear that something about their current way of living or relating to themselves and with others is not working well. They most often have tried very hard to bring about the changes that they are seeking through counselling, medication, lifestyle changes and so on, with no relief and continuing discomfort. They may not have a clear sense of the steps they might take to bring about the changes they are hoping for, or if what they are wanting for their life is even possible. They may be in crisis or seeking a turning point in life. Using the metaphor of journey and identity migration, our work in this phase is preparing persons for the journey they are embarking on and getting a clear sense of where they wish to head. The preparation and separation phase typically unfolds over the course of three sessions.[4] During this time, we work alongside the person to gain a deeper sense of what they are wanting to separate from; for example, problem-saturated stories of isolation, depression or despair, or trauma experiences they have been living and struggling with. It is a time of looking back with care and looking forward with intention.

We begin to linguistically separate the person from the problem and get a sense of the tactics of the problem and the ways it has been operating in their life. We learn about the skills and knowledges they possess, and the people, places, ideas and things that offer them a sense of belonging and hope. We also track and highlight ways in which they have been able to resist the problem's influence within their lives and relationships. There are usually ideas and beliefs that are not serving them that they want to leave behind. Problems thrive by isolating and disconnecting persons from others, estranging them from communities and from themselves. As we move away from seeing problems as "individual" experiences, we can explore how we exist within relational realms of being and recognise who we are in relation to how others perceive us (White, 2007).

During our initial preparation sessions, Fred had a hard time separating his voice from the voice and influence of depression, but he agreed that depression might be an unreliable narrator of his past, present and yet-to-come future. Fred was concerned that, given his long-standing relationship of over 20 years with depression, another style of relationship with himself might be impossible to find.

Some questions I might ask as a person prepares to leave the known and familiar:

- What brings you to seek psychedelic-assisted therapy at this time?

- What can you tell me about what you've been struggling with, pushed around by, oppressed by in your life? What pushback have you encountered in trying to separate yourself from the problem/dilemma?

- In what ways has the problem/dilemma been influencing your life? What plans do you imagine that this problem has for your life? Are you okay with this? Why is/isn't this comfortable for you? If I were to ask a loved one if they were comfortable with how the problem has been mistreating you, what do you imagine that they would say?

- Are there identities, ways of being or ideas and beliefs that are no longer serving you that you want to leave behind? What difference do you imagine this would make?

- Reflecting on our therapeutic conversations, what have you been learning about what matters to you, what is making a difference in your life and relationships, what you give value to, and the kind of future you are imagining for yourself?

Setting intentions and moving towards what matters

Embarking on a major life change and evolution can be unsettling and often involves feelings of loss, sadness, grief, uncertainty and fear. In this phase, persons are preparing to leave a known territory of their life to step into the unknown. It is important to develop a clear understanding of what the person is moving towards, and the hopes and preferences they hold for living a life filled with vitality. In this phase, we explore their ideas about life, including their attitudes towards living, what they give value to, their hopes and preferences, and the ways of being they wish to inhabit.

We also develop and practice skills that persons can use to stay grounded in their body and breath before, during and after the psychedelic-assisted therapy sessions.

Akin to activities like downhill skiing, it is wise to learn some skills of navigating in inner experiential worlds and to be well prepared before beginning to explore the non-ordinary states of awareness that may emerge during the action of psychedelic substances. (Richards, n.d.)

The person may already have knowledge and skills for remaining calm and relaxed in new situations. We can also explore and try out techniques that others have found helpful; for example, the RAIN practice (Brach, 2020) and the 4-7-8 Breath (Weil, 1999). For others, a calm state of mind and body might be cultivated in nature or through cultural teachings, journalling or spending time with persons they love. Experimenting with how the person can connect with a state of calmness and relaxation prior to their psychedelic medicine journey can help prepare them for entering and staying grounded when they enter an altered state of consciousness, which is by its very definition a leaving of the known and familiar.

Psychedelic experiences are influenced by what Timothy Leary called "set and setting" (Hartogsohn, 2017; Leary et al., 1963). *Set* refers to the mindset of the person taking the psychedelic and their intention for the session. Set can be influenced by the person's intention for psychedelic-assisted therapy, their emotional state, and previous experiences with psychoactive substances. *Setting* refers to the physical environment: the therapy room with its sounds, lighting, fragrances, comfort and relative safety.

In the preparation phase, we discuss "set and setting", the timeline of the psychedelic medicine they are taking, and how the session may unfold. We work with the person to help them set their intentions for their psychedelic-assisted therapy session and explore how their intentions, purposes and desires will support them in healing and growth. It is important to acknowledge that intentions may emerge organically from the experience itself. Maintaining a not-knowing stance is essential, as it allows space for new intentions, stories, meanings and knowledges to emerge during the medicine session. An example of a question to support intention setting is "After the medicine session, what would be happening that would make life more wonderful for you?"

From a narrative therapy perspective, creating a sense of safety, both physical and relational, is foundational to psychedelic-assisted work. One way this is supported

is by inviting the person to meet the co-therapist ahead of the medicine session. This typically happens during the third preparation session, when the person, therapist and co-therapist come together in a shared conversation. This helps establish familiarity, trust and a sense of who will be accompanying them in the session ahead.

In the preparation sessions, we discuss whether the person would like to invite their chosen support person, someone from their community, to join them near the end of their medicine session for the early integration conversation. This would take place when the support person arrives to take them home at the end of the day. It is not uncommon for people to want their support person to be present during this time so that parts of their journey that feel significant can be witnessed and honoured. This presence allows the support person to not only witness what has emerged but also to walk alongside the person in what is still unfolding. In group psychedelic therapy, this practice becomes even more resonant, as participants accompany one another through the preparation, medicine journey and reintegration processes, bearing witness to each other's stories and offering recognition and support as each person moves towards a renewed sense of identity, meaning and place in life.

Conversation with Fred

In our preparation sessions, depression took up a lot of space. Fred estimated that depression took up approximately 95% of his thoughts, leaving him a mere 5% of depression-free thinking. Fred and I invited the words of the people he loved and who loved him to help populate the therapy room (Reynolds, 2011). We spoke about the ways his partner could be invited into conversations about possible intentions for his upcoming medicine session, and discussed the idea of grit, which he had learnt from his grandmother, Ruby. We had conversations about what Ruby might have known about grit, how grit could serve a useful ally at this moment, and what Fred's tender conversations with Ruby may have brought to her life.

Below are some questions I ask about aspirations, desires and mindset for the medicine session:[5]

- As you consider your hopes for the psychedelic medicine session, what kind of relationship would you like to be cultivating with yourself, and with the problem or dilemma you're facing? What are some possible intentions that are beginning to show up?

- What do your intentions say about what you hold precious, what you give value to, and your hopes and dreams for your life?

- Viewing your intentions like a compass for your upcoming psychedelic-assisted therapy session: Imagine holding that compass in your hands. Which way does it point, and in what ways might moving in that direction bring you more ease or comfort?

- If your intentions could offer you a new vantage point – one that allows you to see the problem differently and begin to re-author your relationship with it – what would you hope to see?

- Are there things you know about yourself that might make it easier – or harder – to embark on this experience fully? When you think back to times you've tried something unfamiliar, what supported you in leaning into it?

- What are you most concerned about encountering in your psychedelic-assisted therapy session? What strengths and skills do you possess that will support you in navigating those possible encounters?

- If you start feeling worried or concerned, how will you alert me to this? What might I notice, and how could I best support you in those moments?

- Thinking of a person or a creature (perhaps a friend or a pet, living or dead) in your life that you have valued and trusted, what would they tell me about the courage/strength/bravery that could serve you well on this therapeutic journey? Are there any spirit allies or loved ones you would like to introduce me to and invite to accompany you on your journey?

Transition/liminal phase: The psychedelic journey

Crossing the threshold

This phase marks a significant shift: a crossing of the threshold from everyday awareness into an altered state of consciousness. The medicine session marks an entry into the in-between – a threshold space where problem-saturated stories loosen and new knowledges, stories and meanings may be experienced. It can feel like stepping through a doorway into unfamiliar territory, where the usual stories of self may soften, and new sensations, meanings or images begin to take form.

This unfolding is supported by the intentions the person has brought with them, the container of the therapeutic space, and the presence of the therapist and co-therapist, who accompany the person on their journey with care and attentiveness. Rather than directing the experience, the therapists bear witness to what emerges, holding space for the person to meet the unknown with curiosity, courage and connection to what matters most to them.

From a therapeutic perspective, establishing a safe physical setting and mindset for the participant requires that practitioners take an active role in creating an environment that is conducive to the therapeutic experience.

On the day of the psychedelic-assisted therapy session, the person (or persons if participating in a group setting) arrives and is warmly welcomed by the therapist and co-therapist into a ceremonial space where intention and awareness are central and where the psychedelic-assisted therapy session will unfold. This space has been prepared with structure and care, honouring the significance of what is about to begin. Time is taken to settle into the space, reconnect with one's body, and draw on personal practices that support calm and presence.

Together, the therapists and the person review the plan for the day, creating a shared understanding of the journey ahead. This covers the timeline of the medicine they will be taking, the administration process, the journey or immersion phase, the emergence and initial integration period, and finally, space for reflection and return. Mapping out the flow of the day not only offers clarity but also helps foster a sense of safety, trust and shared intention as the person approaches the threshold of the experience. The person is invited to create their "nest" – arranging pillows or a cosy blanket and placing meaningful objects, photos or images nearby to accompany them throughout the journey.

Informed consent and practical safety considerations are reviewed at this point. We discuss how only the therapist and co-therapist will be present during the medicine session, that the space will remain private and uninterrupted, and that they will not be left alone at any point. They are also informed that, in support of their safety and wellbeing, once they have ingested the medicine, the session becomes a held and contained space. This means that, for the duration of the experience, they are asked to remain within the therapeutic setting until their pre-arranged support person arrives to accompany them home. We also have clear conversations and agreements about physical touch, including a reaffirmation that sexual touch will never be part of the therapeutic frame. Each person is invited to express their preferences for touch: whether they would like to give consent for supportive touch, such as a hand on the shoulder or having their hand held if requested during the medicine session, or whether they prefer not to receive any touch at all.

Prior to ingesting the psychedelic medicine, we draw on the person's own knowledge of what helps them feel grounded and relaxed. These practices are not only soothing but also offer a meaningful way to reconnect with their deeply held values, supporting them to settle into the space and attune to themselves. If desired, a candle may be lit to mark the beginning of the process. The person is then invited to speak their intentions and hopes for the medicine session, as crafted during the preparation sessions, often while holding the medicine. This gesture underscores the relational connection they are co-creating between themselves, their intentions and the medicine as a partner in the unfolding journey. When they feel ready, the person ingests the psychedelic. At this point, the therapists may wish to offer a retelling of the participant's hopes and intentions for their medicine journey. They may also offer a song, poem or prayer that resonates with the person's journey, creating a bridge between intention and experience.[6]

A psychedelic music playlist begins playing when the participant arrives, both in the room and later in the person's headphones. A psychedelic playlist is curated to enhance and accompany the person on their psychedelic journey. A playlist for a psilocybin medicine session supports the arc of the medicine (arrival, pre-onset, onset, building or peak intensity of the psilocybin, re-entry and return to normal consciousness) (Thomas, 2024). Bill Richards described the role of the playlist in a psychedelic medicine session:

> I think of it as a nonverbal support system, sort of like the net for a trapeze artist. If all is going well, you're not even aware that the net is there – you don't even hear the music – but if you start getting anxious, or if you need it, it's immediately there to provide a structure. (Bill Richards, as interviewed in Shapiro, 2020)

Typically, I use curated playlists developed specifically for psychedelic therapy, such as the Johns Hopkins Psychedelic Therapy Playlist, originally created by

researchers for psilocybin-assisted sessions. These playlists are structured to support the emotional arc of the experience and are chosen for their neutrality, evocative quality and therapeutic intent (Shapiro, 2020).

Recently, I've begun incorporating a few songs selected by the person to be played towards the end of the session. During our preparation sessions, I invite the person to choose music that holds deep personal meaning: songs that may remind them of a special time in their life, connect them with loved ones, describe a life they wish to live, or that have offered support during difficult moments (see Maund, 2021). These selections often carry emotional resonance and can help gently guide the person back into their life with a feeling of being welcomed with connection and intention.

As the medicine begins to take effect, the person chooses to lie down when they feel ready, with the therapists gently assisting with eyeshades, a weighted blanket or other comforts if requested. Throughout the session, the therapist and co-therapist remain present, bearing witness, offering support and responding to the needs of the moment with attunement and care. The person is supported in entering into and to attuning to a relationship with the experience they co-create with the medicine, turning inward, observing their physical and emotional states, and noticing shifts in perspective as they become increasingly immersed in the psychedelic journey.

Positioning myself as a narrative therapist in a psychedelic-assisted therapy session, I listen for preferred stories, values and knowledges that are named through the experience. I do not see myself as an expert or guide, but as a witness: someone who holds space with care and offers a steady, respectful presence within a safe-enough container (Bird, 2000) for the work to unfold. I attend closely to what resonates deeply for the person and seek to honour the knowledges, wisdoms and meanings that begin to take shape. The person's own intentions, agency and language remain at the centre of the process. Depending on what kind of support is needed, the therapist or co-therapist may write down words the person speaks during the session. We remain present throughout, accompanying them through moments of struggle, sadness, deeply felt knowings or joy. I also listen for "news of difference" and possible "unique outcomes" (White & Epston, 1990) as they arise. For example, if someone who has long spoken to themselves with harshness begins to speak with tenderness or kindness, I may note their words so we can return to them together in a future conversation, if they wish, to support the integration of that shift and explore whether it's something they would like to continue cultivating.

Liminality and early integration

As the medicine experience begins to wear off, a gentle transition is supported by the therapist and co-guide to welcome the person back with grounding presence, soft voices, intentional pacing and comforting offerings such as light snacks, fruit, water or tea. When the person is ready, we gently ask what they wish to share about their experience: what stood out, where they felt transported, or what they feel moved to speak about. This marks the beginning of early integration, where the person may begin to name parts of their journey, not as a report, but as threads of meaning that connect to what matters most to them.

We invite the sharing of any moments, images, questions or emotions that feel significant: those that may have stirred curiosity, touched something important, or opened space for movement. These early stages of integration remind me of Barbara Myerhoff's (1982, 1986) definitional ceremonies and the reflecting team processes described by Tom Andersen (1987) and Michael White (1995). In this spirit, the therapist and co-therapist offer reflections based on what they witnessed, sharing what resonated, what stood out, or how they were moved by what was shared.

Researchers have observed that during medicine sessions, individuals may be in a heightened state of openness and suggestibility due to increased neural plasticity (Carhart-Harris & Nutt, 2017). From a narrative perspective, this underscores the importance of avoiding advice-giving, positive affirmations or premature conclusions (Morgan, 2000; White & Epston, 1990). Rather than interpreting the experience, we hold space for the person's meaning-making – supporting the articulation of emerging understandings that honour the person's agency, values and preferred stories.

Following the session, I document the reflections and curiosities in the form of a narrative letter, which is sent in the days that follow. This letter becomes a further act of witnessing, one that supports the person in staying connected to what is unfolding and the stories they may be beginning to re-author. People often share these letters with family and friends as a way to catch them up on new developments in their lives.

The ceremony closes with intention and care. When the person feels ready, we contact their pre-arranged support person to come and pick them up. If it was previously decided that the support person would be invited into the conversation, the person may choose to share parts of their journey at that time. The support person then accompanies them home, helping to hold space for the continued unfolding of the experience in the days to come.[7]

Betwixt and between

In the hours and days following the journey, the person may continue to dwell in a liminal state. New images, emotions or understandings may begin to take shape, not yet fully formed but rich with possibility. This is a fertile time for reflection and gentle meaning-making, a bridge between the session and life beyond it. The person is invited to write about their experience, if that feels meaningful or supportive to them, and to revisit the playlist as a way of reconnecting with and thickening the felt experience and stories of their journey.

The increased neuroplasticity that occurs with psychedelic use typically lasts from a few days to a month or so after their use (de Vos et al., 2021; Ly et al., 2018). This period offers a valuable window in which intentional integration practices can help consolidate emerging knowledges and support the development of new patterns and preferred ways of being in a person's life (Jones, 2025). Ideally, the first formal integration session should take place a day or two after the psychedelic-assisted therapy session. The person is encouraged to write down the knowings, questions, feelings, sensations, curiosities and ideas they want to hold on to in the days and weeks following the psychedelic-assisted therapy session so they can return to them. If a person feels uncertain about what their experience might mean, we can gently acknowledge the emergent and nonlinear nature of psychedelic journeys (Richards, 2017). Rather than seeking a singular "takeaway", we invite a stance of curiosity and patience, trusting that meaning and understanding may continue to take shape over time, in conversation with their own values, intentions and lived experience.

I find the narrative practice of writing letters to clients to be a meaningful way of supporting their integration process. Here is the letter I sent to Fred after our first integration session.

Dear Fred,

It was such a pleasure meeting with you today. I found myself grinning with delight at the start of our session when you said, "I feel like a huge weight has been lifted off of my shoulders", and "I honestly feel like I can actually think". When you spoke of being able to navigate your thoughts more and being more in touch with "the inner portion of myself that I used to like", I felt myself imagining the relief that you must have felt to be in touch with yourself again. Is relief the right word or is something else? I imagine that words might not do your experiences justice and I am having a hard time expressing the magnitude of the emotions I witnessed and felt in our meeting today and in the medicine sit on Monday.

I found my entire body covered in goosebumps and had tears in my eyes when you said that you feel like you did after 25 or 30 rounds of ECT.[8] Your descriptions of the weight of depression have been so powerful that I am imagining the relief that you might have and be feeling. You said, "not having that pain so in your face, it opens up possibilities. The possibility to not be as crippled. To be vital, to have agency". In our session today, you described connecting with "self-love, compassion for self, and being a flawed human", and said that the okays[9] were an understanding of that.

That you are human.

And the recognition that depression had paved the way for an abusive relationship with yourself, and in doing so made you hold yourself to a higher standard than you would hold others to. You described that relationship and those standards as toxic. I wonder if in the future, should depression try to convince you to hold yourself to a toxic standard again, how self-love, compassion for self, and the knowing that you are a flawed human (and that so is everyone else and that is okay) might prevent depression from doing so.

I also find myself wondering if the okays might continue to be a guide for you as you walk a new path and continue to reconnect with yourself. If the okays that I witnessed you saying to yourself during the medicine sit, okays spoken with a gentleness and care, might become a mantra of sorts: "It's okay. I'm okay. Okay."

You spoke of being both surprised and unprepared for the crushing sadness and emotion that you experienced in the medicine sit. I found myself wondering about what helped you tolerate, be present with and move through the crushing sadness to get to the other side. And I also found myself wondering what the other side was.

I hope you enjoy the music tonight and have a lovely time with your partner.

I am attaching a resource about self-compassion that you might enjoy.[10] There are a lot of different exercises to practice and explore to build the self-compassion muscle. I hope you bathe yourself in it, and in doing so drown out the voice of depression.

In Solidarity,
Christine

I often turn to the metaphor of a rite of passage, as envisioned by Michael White, to help frame the psychedelic therapy process. This image offers a compassionate and grounding way to understand the emotional territory that can unfold after a session. Van Gennep (1960) spoke of individuals in transition as "wavering between two worlds" (p. 18). Turner (1969) described this liminal space as being "betwixt and between". These ideas resonate with many who find themselves feeling suspended – no longer fully rooted in the life they knew, yet not quite landed in what comes next. Naming this phase as part of a larger arc helps normalise the disorientation, vulnerability or heightened openness that can emerge in the days and weeks following a psychedelic experience. It becomes a shared language for navigating change, one that honours both the possibility for discomfort and the potential of the in-between.

Richard Rohr (1999) described how experiences of liminality can make space for transformations, further supporting persons in stepping away from problem identities and evolving towards the development of new preferred identities. Within a liminal space

> we are betwixt and between the familiar and the completely unknown. There alone is our old world left behind, while we are not yet sure of the new existence. That's a good space where genuine newness can begin. Get there often and stay as long as you can by whatever means possible ... This is the sacred space where the old world is able to fall apart, and a bigger world is revealed. If we don't encounter liminal space in our lives, we start idealizing normalcy.
> (Rohr, 1999, pp. 155–156)

In my work, I share the rites of passage metaphor with clients, particularly during the preparation and integration phases of psychedelic-assisted therapy. I describe the process as involving three broad stages: separation from the known, entering a threshold or liminal space, and reincorporating what has been learnt into everyday life. When someone feels disoriented, this framework can act as a map to orient themselves in the experience. I often share that this part of the process, when things feel unsettled or unfamiliar, is not necessarily a sign that something is wrong, but may indicate that they are in a middle space, where the dominant story has loosened and the preferred story is still taking shape.

Using this metaphor in conversation can invite curiosity and self-compassion. It also provides a shared language for understanding transformation as a process, not a single insight or outcome. Persons have expressed that naming this "in-between" phase helps them stay connected to the work unfolding, even when clarity hasn't yet arrived.

This stage often brings confusion and uncertainty. Clients may need reminders to slow down, be gentle with themselves, and make room for not-knowing. I invite them to stay close to the shifts that arise, whether a felt sense of connection, a new perspective or a moment of clarity, and to remain curious about what new possibilities these experiences might open up.

I find it helpful to encourage persons to listen to, and lean in to, any "teachings", "sense of connection", "perspective shifts", "aha moments", or "deeply felt knowings" that they experienced during their psychedelic-assisted therapy session. When people make a leap, experience epiphanies, or take small steps in breaking from debilitating and restraining

patterns and stepping away from problem identities or lifestyles, they are often confronted with the challenges of how to begin to live in new ways. This often requires learning new ways of living and relating, and re-evaluating values and preferences. This can involve trying out new ways of being, re-evaluating what matters, and developing new skills or understandings to support these shifts.

Often, people describe being in an in-between space – clear that their previous ways of living no longer serve them, and sensing where they might like to move towards, but not yet having the support, resources or language to step into these new ways or moments of being. Until these new ways of being are named, practiced and lived into, this transitional space can feel unsettling. In these moments, a supportive community of concern is especially helpful, as others in their lives may not yet recognise or support the changes they are moving towards. In psychedelic-assisted therapeutic work, people often depart from the familiar into the unknown, and then return to their everyday surroundings with novel and innovative ideas and a heartening sense of "how to go on". They are tasked with determining how to incorporate these new ways of being into their present day. After a medicine session, a person may experience separation from past ways of thinking or acting, or they may have a pause available to them that they did not have access to before. Persons may find themselves catapulted out of long-standing beliefs, patterns and ways of being.

Questions to scaffold and support these changes may include:

- What have you noticed that feels unfamiliar or unexpected since the medicine session?

- Was there a moment where you responded differently than you might have in the past?

- What stood out about that experience?

In the immediate days after his psilocybin-assisted therapy session, Fred described feeling like a huge weight had been lifted off of his shoulders. He said, "I honestly feel like I can actually think, allowing me to navigate my thoughts more, and be more in touch with the inner portion of myself that I used to like".

For some people, the psychedelic experience can impart a sense of oneness and highlight the interconnectedness of all beings (Fadiman, 2011). Such a relational experience may allow for openings to move towards stories of co-creation, embedding our lives with others, creating a sense of community and belonging with others (Watts et al., 2022) in ways previously unimagined nor experienced. Questions to ask to elicit such stories may include:

- Are there relationships or communities that feel newly important – or differently important – after what you've experienced?

- If the experience showed you something about the kind of friend, partner, parent or community member you want to be, what did it show you?

- How would you describe the kind of relationships you hope to cultivate going forward?

- What would it mean for you to live more of your life from that place of connection or belonging?

I have been present in psychedelic medicine sessions in which people have described a shift in how they understood their experiences and their ways of being in the world, often accompanied by a new sense of compassion. Such shifts allow for the development of a preferred relationship with oneself and a sense of personal agency as the person begins to steer towards new, preferred territories of living. While the psychedelic may open a window or create conditions for this shift, it is often the meaning-making a person does in relation to their experience that shapes lasting change.

The therapist's role is to support this meaning-making process, helping to scaffold reflection, language and story around what is emerging so that these shifts can be integrated into the person's life in intentional and sustaining ways. An example of this is when I was co-facilitating a brief group sharing circle immediately after a psychedelic-assisted therapy session. A person who had experienced many deaths and losses in their family and community described having witnessed themself digging a grave. They described a feeling of deep sadness come over them as they began to wonder "now who has died?" Then they spoke of recognising that no-one had died. Rather, they were digging a grave for the beliefs and ideas they had been carrying that were no longer serving them. This emerging understanding became a central focus of their integration work, an intentional process of making meaning from their experience and exploring how to support a life more aligned with their values and preferred ways of being. They began to get to know themselves as a person who no longer had to carry the weight of beliefs that had previously limited them, and who could now begin stepping into ways of living that felt more congruent with what mattered most to them.

In this example, psychedelic-assisted therapy offered a space where problems could be seen in new ways, and where a restoration of personal agency became possible. While the medicine may have opened access to new perspectives or emotional experiences, it was through the person's meaning-making and reflective engagement that they began to experience some separation from previously dominant problem narratives. This externalising shift – co-constructed through their interpretation of the experience – created a renewed sense of possibility, opening a path forward that was more aligned with their values and preferred direction in life.

These questions may be asked of people in betwixt and between states and the early integration phase:

- What resonated for you most during the psychedelic-assisted therapy session? How does this connect to what you most give value to and hopes/dreams/preferences for your life and relationships?

- At any point in your psychedelic-assisted therapy session, did you begin to "feel" a counter story? Were there ways that you experienced the psychedelic externalising the problem/dilemma, and if so, what new understandings are you now carrying?

- How did your intentions show up during the psychedelic-assisted therapy session?

- If you find yourself feeling untethered in moments, what are practices that you can use to tether or ground yourself?

- If there was pain/sadness during the psychedelic-assisted therapy session, what was that pain in relation to? What did you see, feel or hear that touched on a longing? What did you learn about how that pain might want to be tended to?

Reincorporation/integration phase: Weaving new meaning into daily life

After the psychedelic-assisted therapy session, the person may begin to develop a clearer road map for the direction they want their life to head in. They may have gained distance from thinking patterns or ways of being that felt rigid and cemented, or they may have a clearer sense of how the problem has been working in their lives.

However, the psychedelic experience is not a magic pill that dissolves all problems or dilemmas. Rather, it may open a window of possibility, one that requires effort, reflection and practice to translate into lasting change. The integration phase, or what White (1997) referred to as reincorporation, involves returning to daily life with the task of weaving emerging reflections and preferred ways of being into everyday choices, relationships and routines. This is often where the hard work lies. Like learning a new skill, it requires intention and repetition, practicing new ways of thinking, noticing when old patterns reappear, and actively choosing actions that reflect the values and preferences the person is stepping into. Without these efforts, even powerful experiences can fade without becoming embedded in lived experience.

In the weeks after his psilocybin session, Fred realised that depression exists best in certainty: black or white and all-or-nothing thinking. In our therapy sessions, we played with the idea of staying in the "grey" and being alert to when depression was promising certainty. Fred began to speak to some close friends and family members about his experience as he also recognised that depression feeds off silence. He described how during the AIDS crisis in the 1980s, there was a saying: "Silence = Death". He felt that this applied to depression as well. After our session, I looked this saying up and discovered it was used as a consciousness-raising rallying cry by activists to engage communities to demand political action, medical research and pharmaceutical support for those suffering and dying from AIDS (Kerr, 2017). In our next session, we spoke of how our community needs a similar rallying cry against depression, and began imagining what that might look like.

In our preparation work together, Fred had already begun the process of externalising his relationship with depression and viewing it as something separate from who he is. Following the psychedelic experience, this distinction seemed to land in a more embodied and convincing way. Through the meaning he made of what emerged in the session, Fred was able to further separate his preferred identity from the identity that depression had imposed. This allowed him to reclaim his voice, quiet the influence of depression, and begin moving towards relationships and ways of living that felt more aligned with his values.

After psychedelic-assisted therapy sessions, I have witnessed others similarly describing how certain thoughts, actions or urges no longer held the same pull, or even seem to *disappear*[11] (Pollan, 2018). In this case, integration work involves actively supporting the development of more intentional, values-aligned ways of living that reflect the person's preferred direction.

The integration phase involves supporting individuals to incorporate the insights and preferred ways of being that emerged during psychedelic-assisted therapy into their daily lives. White (1997) described a similar idea through the metaphor of "reincorporation", which offers therapeutic affordances for exploring a renewed sense of identity and belonging.

> Reincorporation is achieved when a person finds that they've arrived at another place in life, where they experience a "fit" that provides for them a sense of once again being at home with themselves and with a way of life. At this time, persons regain a sense of being knowledgeable and skilled in matters of living. (White, 1997, p. 4)

Questions I have asked to assist with integration and strengthening a preferred story have included:

- What did you see/learn/know/feel/hear during and following the session and in the days/weeks after that contributed to a sense of not being fatally flawed? Since no longer viewing yourself as fatally flawed, what have you noticed is different in the way that you have been thinking about yourself and the events of your life?

- Since having this new understanding of yourself, what have you been noticing about the ways that depression operates in your life? Have you been able to see depression's tactics more clearly?

- What difference will seeing depression from this vantage point make as you step towards preferred territories of living and living a life of vitality?

- What has been most influential in your continuing move away from depression's clutches and your sense of knowing how to proceed?

- What difference will this new understanding about yourself make in your life? What might this new understanding allow you to do that you've never done before?

- Where has this psychedelic-assisted therapy experience taken you to, and what understandings have you come to that you might not otherwise have arrived at?

Hazards and comebacks

In some of the psychedelic-assisted therapy work I've been involved in, the changes experienced during sessions have not been as enduring as the person had hoped. This highlights the importance of viewing psychedelics not as a cure, but as one part of a broader therapeutic process. For some, the experience feels profoundly transformative; for others, continued therapeutic support – including additional psychedelic therapy sessions – has been necessary to sustain and build on emerging shifts.

It is common to encounter stumbling blocks, and many people need to revisit some of the work done in earlier phases in order to move forwards once again in their preferred direction. During preparation, it is important to be clear about the possible hazards and setbacks the person may encounter. For example, when persons are first consulting us about this work, it is important to stress the importance of both the preparation and the integration work that needs to be done prior to and following the psychedelic-assisted therapy session. It is also important to discuss the concept of a "betwixt and between" phase, in which one's familiar sense of being in the world is absent, and where nothing means quite what it did before. If persons are prepared for this liminality, then they are better able to make a plan for how to best take care of themselves should they be confronted with it.

When working with persons who are trying to break free from an addiction or are on a journey to develop a new relationship with a problem, it is our duty as practitioners to prepare them for the possibility that the problem may try to make a comeback in their lives. Otherwise, the problem can attempt to convince them that they will never be able to change, that they will never escape depression's clutches, that because this did not "work" nothing will work, or that it is their fault because they "did something wrong" in the psychedelic-assisted medicine session.

Possible questions that can be asked to illuminate potential hazards or comebacks include:

- What might you notice should old ways of being and old patterns of thinking begin to reappear? What would be the first sign that this was happening, and what are some possible responses that you could enact to resist the problem's attempted comeback?

- Thinking of the problem or dilemma as wanting to retain its grip on you, what do you imagine that the problem is making of the space that you have created that has been keeping it at bay?

- Moving forward, what is most important for you to pay attention to? What is the work you imagine still needs to be done?

- In times of uncertainty or discomfort, how might the compassion that you experienced in your psychedelic-assisted medicine session be a resource to you to support you in times when the problem is trying to make a comeback in your life?

- You described having access to a space between responding and reacting, a pause that was not available to you prior to the psychedelic-assisted therapy session. How might this pause support you in responding in new and preferred ways to the problem or dilemma?

Conclusion

This paper is directed towards practitioners already engaged in psychedelic-assisted work. It outlines what narrative therapy has to offer them, both as a set of practices and as an orientation that can deepen and sustain their work. When working from a narrative therapy approach, in which meaning is co-created and lives are understood to be multi-storied, psychedelic experiences can create conditions that support the emergence of previously marginalised or subordinate storylines. Psychedelic experiences may allow individuals to reconnect with unique outcomes and preferred purposes, intentions, desires and identities that the problem story may have obscured. In the context of psychedelic-assisted therapy, it is not the medicine alone that brings about this shift, but the ways people engage with their experience, reflect on its meanings, and are supported to give language to what matters to them. This collaborative process can help breathe life back into a sense of connectedness, compassion and agency. It may offer a new vantage point from which a person can begin to see the problem differently – and from there, choose to re-author their relationship with it.

In a narrative therapy approach, identity is viewed as being socially created within a community of others. When people become socially isolated by problems, they may lose access to the relationships and conversations that create space for new and preferred stories of their lives to be constructed, leaving only the problem to shape the story. People get lost when they don't have a narrative they can move forward with, so they continue to reproduce the known and familiar. A therapeutic psychedelic medicine session can be a bridge from the known and familiar into another realm where persons are able to glimpse, feel and experience how it may be possible for them to be living in the world. A re-peopling of identity and a sense of continuity allows people to step into other possibilities. It allows for the restoration of personal agency and gives a sense of how to go on with one's life. It lends agency and choice to the direction they and their life are headed in. I feel honoured to be able to collaborate therapeutically with struggling others utilising psychedelics and as a narrative therapist witnessing the newfound hope persons experience.

Acknowledgments

I would like to acknowledge the people who read earlier drafts of this paper and offered helpful feedback. I would like to thank Jeff Zimmerman, Todd May and especially Colin James Sanders for reading and re-reading many drafts of this paper.

Notes

1 This paper describes psychedelic-assisted therapy using psilocybin and ketamine. The ketamine work was done with a team of registered nurses, psychiatrist, medical doctor, myself and one other registered clinical counsellor. The psilocybin work was done in a team comprising a psychiatrist, myself and one other registered clinical counsellor.

2 The psychedelic protocols described in this paper are adapted from the MAPS protocols developed by Michael Mithoefer (2017) and taught in the MAPS MDMA-assisted therapy training program. It is important to note that the psychedelic therapy protocols described in this paper use relatively high doses of psychedelics. There are other protocols currently in use, for example psycholytic therapy, which uses lower doses of psychedelics combined with psychotherapy often over multiple sessions (Passie et al., 2022), and sacramental protocols, which emphasise spiritual insights (Baker, 2005).

3 Seeing this as a deliberate act of resistance, we could say that Fred had become refractory to the psychiatric medicines he had been prescribed.

4 Persons coming in for SAP-approved therapy may not have had prior experience with re-authoring conversations. Narrative ideas and practices are introduced to them in the three preparation sessions (more sessions can be added if wanted by the person). For others, we may have had many re-authoring conversations prior to embarking in psychedelic-assisted psychotherapy.

5 These questions evoke "re-membering conversations" (Hedtke, 2012; White, 2007), which represent an important line of inquiry in narrative therapy.

> Re-membering conversations are shaped by the conception that identity is founded upon an "association of life" rather than on a core self. This association of life has a membership composed of the significant figures and identities of a person's past, present, and projected future, whose voices are influential with regard to the construction of the person's identity. (White, 2007, p. 128)

6 In the preparation sessions, we ask about any favourite poems, meaningful phrases or prayers that the person finds comforting or grounding – something they would like to have read or spoken aloud on the day of their medicine journey.

7 The support person is given a handout about supporting their loved one after a psychedelic therapy medicine session, along with a link to the playlist that was used during the session.

8 Fred had undergone many treatments in an effort to address the effects of treatment-resistant depression, a long and difficult journey that included 25 to 30 rounds of electroconvulsive therapy (ECT) before he noticed any significant improvement in mood. After just one session of psilocybin-assisted therapy, he shared that his mood felt as improved as it had following the entire course of ECT

9 During the medicine session, Fred repeated the word "okay" many times, each time with noticeable kindness and gentleness. It was as if he was getting to know something in those moments, each "okay" felt thoughtful and intentional. In the letter I wrote to him afterward, I included this detail, as I was curious about whether it held any significance for him and how he made sense of those moments.

10 https://self-compassion.org/exercise-6-self-compassion-journal/

11 For example, Lugo-Radillo and Cortes-Lopez (2021) reported a patient whose Y-BOCS score (a measure of the severity of obsessive-compulsive symptoms) dropped from severe to near remission within 48 hours of psilocybin treatment, with symptoms remaining low 12 weeks after the session. A retrospective survey of 174 adults with OCD also found psychedelic use was associated with significant symptom reduction in obsessions and compulsions.

References

Andersen, T. (1987). The reflecting team: Dialogue and Andersen, T. (1987). The reflecting team: Dialogue and meta-dialogue in clinical work. *Family Process, 26,* 415–428. https://doi.org/10.1111/j.1545-5300.1987.00415.x

Baker, R. (2005). Psychedelic sacraments. *Journal of Psychoactive Drugs, 37*(2), 179–187. https://doi.org/10.1080/02791072.2005.10399799

Bird, J. (2000). *The heart's narrative: Therapy and navigating life's contradictions.* Edge Press.

Brach, T. (2020). *Radical compassion: Learning to love yourself and your world with the practice of RAIN.* Penguin Life.

Carhart-Harris, R., Giribaldi, B., Watts, R., Baker-Jones, M., Murphy-Beiner, A., Murphy, R., Martell, J., Blemings, A., Erritzoe, D., & Nutt, D. J. (2021). Trial of psilocybin versus escitalopram for depression. *New England Journal of Medicine, 384*(15), 1402–1411. https://doi.org/10.1056/nejmoa2032994

Carhart-Harris, R. L., & Nutt, D. J. (2017). *Serotonin and brain function: A tale of two receptors. Journal of Psychopharmacology, 31*(9), 1091–1120. https://doi.org/10.1177/0269881117725915

Carod-Artal, F. J. (2015). Hallucinogenic drugs in pre-Columbian Mesoamerican cultures. *Neurología, 30*(1), 42–49. https://doi.org/10.1016/j.nrl.2011.07.003

Celidwen, Y., Redvers, N., Githaiga, C., Caler, A. J., Sánchez, M. A. A., Fernandez, T. V., Johnson, B. J., & Sacbajá, A. (2022). Ethical principles of traditional Indigenous medicine to guide Western psychedelic research and practice. *The Lancet Regional Health – Americas, 18,* 100410. https://doi.org/10.1016/j.lana.2022.100410

de Vos, C. M. H., Mason, N. L., & Kuypers, K. P. C. (2021). *Psychedelics and neuroplasticity: A systematic review unraveling the biological underpinnings of psychedelic-induced changes in neuroplasticity. Frontiers in Psychiatry, 12,* 724606. https://doi.org/10.3389/fpsyt.2021.724606

Fadiman, J. (2011). *The psychedelic explorer's guide: Safe, therapeutic, and sacred journeys.* Simon and Schuster.

Gerber, K., Flores, I. G., Ruiz, A. C., Ali, I., Ginsberg, N. L., & Schenberg, E. E. (2021). Ethical concerns about psilocybin intellectual property. *ACS Pharmacology and Translational Science, 4*(5), 573–577. https://doi.org/10.1021/acsptsci.0c00171

Griffiths, R. R., Johnson, M. W., Carducci, M. A., Umbricht, A., Richards, W. A., Richards, B. D., Cosimano, M. P., & Klinedinst, M. A. (2016). Psilocybin produces substantial and sustained decreases in depression and anxiety in patients with life-threatening cancer: A randomized double-blind trial. *Journal of Psychopharmacology, 30*(12), 1181–1197. https://doi.org/10.1177/0269881116675513

Hartogsohn, I. (2017). Constructing drug effects: A history of set and setting. *Drug Science, Policy and Law,* (3), 1–17. https://doi.org/10.1177/2050324516683325

Hedtke, L. (2012). Bereavement *support groups: Breathing life into stories of the dead.* Taos Institute.

Johnson, M. W., Richards, W. A., & Griffiths, R. R. (2008). Human hallucinogen research: Guidelines for safety. *Journal of Psychopharmacology, 22*(6), 603–620. https://doi.org/10.1177/0269881108093587

Jones, J. L. (2025). Harnessing neuroplasticity with psychoplastogens: The essential role of psychotherapy in psychedelic treatment optimization. *Frontiers in Psychiatry, 16,* https://doi.org/10.3389/fpsyt.2025.1565852

Kerr, T. (2017, June 20). How six NYC activists changed history with "Silence = Death": The collective that created the Silence = Death poster is back after thirty years to recall its origins and launch new art. *Village Voice.* https://www.villagevoice.com/how-six-nyc-activists-changed-history-with-silence-death/

Leary, T., Litwin, G. H., & Metzner, R. (1963). Reactions to psilocybin administered in a supportive environment. *Journal of Nervous and Mental Disease, 137,* 561–573. https://doi.org/10.1097/00005053-196312000-00007

Lugo-Radillo, A., & Cortes-Lopez, J. L. (2021). Long-term amelioration of OCD symptoms in a patient with chronic consumption of psilocybin-containing mushrooms. *Journal of Psychoactive Drugs, 53*(2), 146–148. https://doi.org/10.1080/02791072.2020.1849879

Ly, C., Greb, A. C., Cameron, L. P., Wong, J. M., Barragan, E. V., Wilson, P. C., Burbach, K. F., Zarandi, S. S., Sood, A., Paddy, M. R., Duim, W. C., Dennis, M. Y., McAllister, A. K., Ori-McKenney, K. M., Gray, J. A., & Olson, D. E. (2018). Psychedelics promote structural and functional neural plasticity. *Cell Reports, 23*(11), 3170–3182. https://doi.org/10.1016/j.celrep.2018.05.022

Maund, I. (2021). Using the Soundtrack of your Life to engage with young people. *International Journal of Therapy and Community Work,* (3), 18–29.

Mithoefer, M. C. (2017, May 22). *A manual for MDMA-assisted psychotherapy in the treatment of posttraumatic stress disorder* (Version 8.1) [Treatment manual]. Multidisciplinary Association for Psychedelic Studies. https://s3-us-west-1.amazonaws.com/mapscontent/research-archive/mdma/TreatmentManual_MDMAAssistedPsychotherapyVersion+8.1_22+Aug2017.pdf

Morgan, A. (2000). *What is narrative therapy? An easy-to-read introduction.* Dulwich Centre Publications.

Multidisciplinary Association for Psychedelic Studies. (2019, May 24). *Statement: Public announcement of ethical violation by former MAPS-sponsored investigators.* https://maps.org/2019/05/24/statement-public-announcement-of-ethical-violation-by-former-maps-sponsored-investigators/

Multidisciplinary Association for Psychedelic Studies. (2021a, January 7). *MAPS code of ethics for psychedelic psychotherapy* (Version 4). https://maps.org/wp-content/uploads/2022/06/MAPS_Psychedelic_Assisted_Psycho-therapy_Code_of_Ethics_V4_22_June_2022_Final.pdf

Multidisciplinary Association for Psychedelic Studies. (2021b, October 20). *Regarding recent allegations of sexual harm in the psychedelic community*. MAPS. https://maps.org/2021/10/20/grecentallegationsofsexualharminthepsychediccommunity

Myerhoff, B. (1982). Life history among the elderly: Performance, visibility and re-membering. In J. Ruby (Ed.), *A crack in the mirror: Reflexive perspectives in anthropology* (pp. 99–117). University of Pennsylvania Press.

Myerhoff, B. (1986). Life not death in Venice: Its second life. In V. Turner & E. Bruner (Eds.), *The anthropology of experience* (pp. 261–286). University of Illinois Press.

Passie, T., Guss, J., & Krähenmann, R. (2022). Lower-dose psycholytic therapy – A neglected approach. *Frontiers in Psychiatry, 13*, 1020505. https://doi.org/10.3389/fpsyt.2022.1020505

Pollan, M. (2018). *How to change your mind: What the new science of psychedelics teaches us about consciousness, dying, addiction, depression, and transcendence.* Penguin Press.

Pollan, M. (2021). *This is your mind on plants.* Penguin Press.

Reynolds, V. (2011, August). *Supervision of solidarity practices: Solidarity teams and people-ing-the-room. Context, 116,* 4–7.

Richards, W. A. (n.d.). Psychedelics in psychotherapy. *Psychwire.* https://psychwire.com/free-resources/q-and-a/1496whe/psychedelics-in-psychotherapy.

Richards, W. A. (2017). Psychedelic psychotherapy: Insights from 25 years of research. *Journal of Humanistic Psychology, 57*(4), 323–337. https://doi.org/10.1177/0022167816670996

Rohr, R. (1999). *Everything belongs: The gift of contemplative prayer.* Crossroad.

Samorini, G. (2019). The oldest archaeological data evidencing the relationship of Homo sapiens with psychoactive plants: A worldwide overview. *Journal of Psychedelic Studies, 3*(2), 63–79. https://doi.org/10.1556/2054.2019.008

Shapiro, M. (2020, October 9). Inside the Johns Hopkins psilocybin playlist. *Dome.* https://www.hopkinsmedicine.org/news/articles/2020/10/inside-the-johns-hopkins-psilocybin-playlist

Siff, S. (2018). R. Gordon Wasson and the publicity campaign to introduce magic mushrooms to mid-century America. *Revue Française d'Études Américaines, 156*(4), 91–105. https://doi.org/10.3917/rfea.156.0091

Thomas, K. (2024, April 17). A psychedelic researcher's approach to creating a psilocybin session playlist. *MAPS Bulletin, 34*(1). https://maps.org/news/bulletin/creating-psilocybin-session-playlist/

Turner, V. (1969). *The ritual process: Structure and anti-structure.* Aldine Publishing.

van Gennep, A. (1960). *The rites of passage: A classic study of cultural celebrations.* University of Chicago Press.

Wasson, R. G. (1957, May 13). Seeking the magic mushroom. *Life,* 100–120.

Watts, R., Day, C., Krzanowski, J., Nutt, D., & Carhart-Harris, R. (2022). The Watts Connectedness Scale: A new three-dimensional scale to measure felt connection in psychedelic research. *Psychopharmacology, 239*(11), 3281–3295. https://doi.org/10.1007/s00213-022-06187-5

Weil, A. (1999). *Breathing: The master key to self healing* [Audiobook CD]. Sounds True.

White, M. (1995). *Re-authoring lives: Interviews and essays.* Dulwich Centre Publications.

White, M. (1997). Challenging the culture of consumption: Rites of passage and communities of acknowledgement. *Dulwich Centre Newsletter,* (2&3), 38–47.

White, M. (2007). *Maps of narrative practice.* Norton.

White, M., & Epston, D. (1990). *Narrative means to therapeutic ends.* Norton.

Solidarity conversations:

A feminist narrative lens on bulimia and abuse

by Kassandra Pedersen

Born in Denmark to a Danish father and a Greek immigrant mother, Kassandra now makes her home in Greece. Kassandra is a psychologist, narrative therapist and supervisor. Her practice is grounded in the values and ethics of narrative therapy, intersectional feminism and social justice frameworks. She works alongside people and communities in ways that invite anti-oppressive pathways, movements and possibilities. Kassandra currently works in private practice across a range of roles including narrative counselling, creative group work and supervision. In addition, she regularly tutors, teaches and facilitates narrative workshops across therapeutic and academic fields. For many years, Kassandra has engaged in co-research with individuals, couples and families on experiences of trauma, gendered and family violence and abuse, grief, mental health concerns, relationship challenges, addiction and anorexia/bulimia, which she approaches with an insider perspective. Kassandra is an Honorary Clinical Fellow of the School of Social Work, The University of Melbourne, and has been tutoring in the Master of Narrative Therapy and Community Work since 2018. She is also part of the teaching faculty at Dulwich Centre and serves as the key faculty member of The Institute of Narrative Therapy (Greece). Kassandra thoroughly enjoys exploring and stretching narrative therapy through non-extractive and decolonial approaches to engaging with lived experience across therapeutic conversations, supervision and teaching. Beyond her work in narrative practice, Kassandra is a former professional cellist and enjoys travelling, swimming and discovering new food experiences. kassandrapedersen@gmail.com https://kassandrapedersen.gr/en/

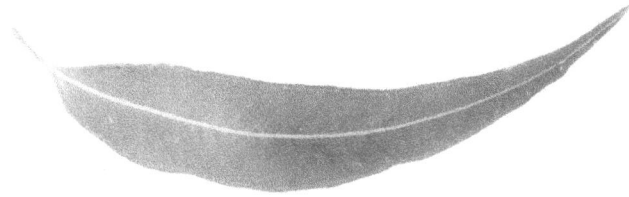

Pedersen, K. (2025). Solidarity conversations: A feminist narrative lens on bulimia and abuse. *International Journal of Narrative Therapy and Community Work*, (2), 49–60. https://doi.org/10.4320/XMNT9956

Author pronouns: she/her

Abstract

Literature often frames bulimia through biomedical models of disease, emphasising biological, psychological and behavioural deficits, and treatments focused on symptom reduction. This paper reimagines so-called "bulimic episodes" as potential acts of testimony or protest against multiple structures of oppression. Drawing on feminist, narrative therapy and anti-oppressive frameworks, I propose an alternative language to bulimic episodes, using the metaphor of tides as a way of redefining bulimia. Application of this metaphor demonstrates how stepping away from conventional conceptualisations affects what is possible in therapeutic conversations. Through my own lived experiences with bulimia and in vitro fertilisation, I examine how medicalisation can reduce agency by centring body-focused narratives, particularly those emphasising weight policing and body image regulation. I also argue that prioritising externalising conversations when bulimia raises its tides can unintentionally replicate neoliberal discourses of food and body management. By expanding the ethics of externalising practices, I propose a nuanced, justice-informed approach that incorporates the "absent but implicit". This perspective moves away from battle metaphors and from dichotomies of "oppressor" and "survivor", which dominate traditional recovery narratives, including some feminist cultural models of eating disorders. Instead, I invite possibilities for navigating people's fluid and varying relationship with bulimia while engaging with other meaningful aspects of their lives. Through a detailed story of practice, this paper offers alternative therapeutic pathways to respond to bulimia's tides. These are grounded in feminist ethics, encouraging agency, solidarity and multi-layered understandings of bulimia.

Key words: bulimia; eating; feminism; absent but implicit; lived experience; co-research; solidarity; narrative therapy; narrative practice

Pedersen, K. (2025). Solidarity conversations: A feminist narrative lens on bulimia and abuse. *International Journal of Narrative Therapy and Community Work*, (2), 49–60. https://doi.org/10.4320/XMNT9956

Author pronouns: she/her

I write from a place where lived experience, therapy and supervision converge – where personal stories become political and intersect with broader structures of oppression (Reynolds, 2013). My approach is shaped by:

- my own experience with bulimia and finding solace through receiving narrative therapy responses crafted to my specific context and location of experience[1]

- my role as a narrative practitioner working with people reclaiming their lives from bulimia

- my work as a supervisor supporting practitioners who respond to people's eating concerns.

My use of "I" in this paper acknowledges the partial and subjective nature of my perspective, shaped by my lived experience, supervision and feminist praxis (Hanisch, 1969). When I use the term "we", this is not to overlook differences among practitioners but to highlight the shared values I treasure in narrative therapy, including social justice, feminism and intersectional principles. This collective stance is held with awareness of the complexity, uncertainty and diversity within both counselling and lived experiences.

Lived experience of bulimia, in vitro fertilisation and the medical gaze

After 15 years of living with bulimia[2], I dove into the world of in vitro fertilisation (IVF) with the excitement of a child opening a birthday gift, only to find my identity reduced to a collection of data points and rigid standards, especially the body mass index (BMI). The medical gaze, as described by Foucault (1973), turned me into a walking chart, aligning my worth with physical criteria and numbers. This scrutiny had me questioning the very definition of "good health", especially at the intersection of fertility, eating disorders and mental health. My IVF consultations felt like a never-ending game of "fix my body", ignoring the nuanced relationship between bulimia and motherhood.

Much of my work takes place in Greece, where culture often idealises motherhood as involving unceasing devotion to the role. Yet beneath the surface, these ideals carry undercurrents of strain and contradiction. In therapeutic conversations, bulimia's tides often draw these tensions into sharper view, revealing the complexity of what lies beneath the idealised image. Through its shifting movements, bulimia repeatedly claims time, energy and space, disrupting life's rhythms and challenging normative ideals of motherhood. Bulimia thrives on dichotomies that position femininities as either destined for motherhood or not, sowing doubts about identity, capacity and purpose – doubts I have deeply felt myself. As a result, I encountered bulimia raising its tides in my life in ways I had never seen before.

The concept of gender performativity[3] was introduced by feminist theorist Judith Butler (1990). In my experience, reproductive normativity – framing maternal success as central to a woman's value – added an extra layer of discursive labour as I felt compelled to continuously "perform" my worth beyond the narrow confines of maternal success. This intersection of health, gender and reproduction highlights how societal norms both shape and constrain women's experiences in ways that are deeply personal yet politically significant.

Medicalised ideas of "healthism", which define wellbeing through health metrics (Crawford, 1980; Hamann, 2009), recruited me into treating my body like a do-it-yourself project. I've never been one to do things halfway, so this perspective led to a single-storied account of my relationship with my body, primarily focused on control.

Thrown deep into the medicalised ocean, I found myself searching for the feminist ideas I treasure and have worked with for years. How is it that we become disconnected from such meaningful knowledge? Even as I share my lived experience in this paper, I find my language occasionally drifting into medicalised culture. This reflection led me to reconnect with supportive feminist spaces and voices (e.g., Braidotti, 2006; Hanisch, 1969; hooks, 1984), which continue to remind me that solutions are not solely an individual's responsibility (Denborough, 2008).

In this writing, I carry the stories of many women, from both counselling and my communities, whose insights have shaped and inspired this paper.[4] Having faced front-on the intersection of medical encounters and bulimia, I aimed to become more attuned to those moments when bulimia raises its head and how we might resist replicating medicalised responses in our conversations. This journey reaffirms that personal experience deeply informs professional practice (C. White & Hales, 1997).

Navigating externalisation with special care

I am profoundly appreciative of narrative practitioners (including Epston et al., 1995; Lainson, 2016; Madigan & Epston, 1995; Maisel et al., 2004; M. White, 2011; M. White & Epston, 1990) for their robust framework for addressing eating concerns. Their detailed descriptions of narrative practices offer valuable insights into the complexities and political dimensions of this work. Michael White and David Epston's concept of externalisation – viewing the problem as separate from the person – has been revolutionary in addressing bulimia by shifting focus from the individual to the problem. Bulimia has its own history of how it becomes established within a person's life, and externalising conversations, along with deconstruction, can create space for co-researching this history and exposing related abuses of power and privilege (M. White, 2007). However, I approach this practice with special care specifically when people describe critical moments of bulimia's tides receding.

Relationships with bulimia are multi-storied, multi-layered, fluid and complex. A unique aspect of bulimia, distinct from anorexia, is its cyclical nature: it is marked by waves of intensity often tied to specific moments in time. Bulimia is not a fixed, singular story but resembles a turbulent tide: sometimes crashing in with overwhelming force, other times quietly receding, leaving us to grapple with its aftermath.

At their highest surge, these so-called "bulimic episodes" resemble a tidal wave, sweeping across the landscape of life and disrupting nearly everything in its path. By suggesting the metaphor of tides in this paper, I hope to acknowledge the ongoing movement of these waves – an aspect often oversimplified or overshadowed by symptom-focused improvement discourses.

Through therapeutic conversations with people living with bulimia, I have noticed that relationships with bulimia are not static. Even when we are not fully immersed by bulimia's waves, we remain aware that we are swimming in the same waters. Bulimia is not something we either "have" or "don't have". This understanding has deepened my interest in therapeutic conversations that go beyond responding to bulimia's explicit operations. Instead, I'm interested in understanding how people ascribe meaning to their experiences while navigating the changing and subtle tides of bulimia.

This paper focuses on a specific moment: when the tide is just beginning to recede.

The aftermath of a wave of bulimia can feel like standing amidst the wreckage of a tsunami: physically, emotionally, mentally and spiritually overwhelmed by the sheer intensity of the experience. Being stuck in the aftermath of bulimia's tempest often involves grappling with its far-reaching implications, such as weight concerns, health issues, bodily dislocation or displacement, and feeling like hostages in our own bodies (Pedersen, 2016). These challenges can intertwine with struggles in relationships, heightened anxiety, suicidality and an overwhelming sense of powerlessness, hopelessness and failure. Many describe feeling trapped in a "liminal space" (M. White, 1997) in which the familiar sense of self and body is disrupted and meanings are in flux. This concept draws on Michael White's use of rites of passage to describe a migration of identity – an anthropological metaphor inspired by Turner (1969) and van Gennep (1909/1960). White applied this idea in his work with women leaving relationships marked by violence and control and in supporting individuals transforming their relationships with alcohol or drugs (Hegarty et al., 2010; M. White, 2000). Central to a rite of passage is the liminal phase – a transitional state between separation and reintegration – in which one is neither entirely anchored in an old identity nor fully integrated into a new one. For those of us navigating bulimia's surges, imagining these as a liminal phase can resonate deeply. They represent a period of turbulence, confusion and even despair as we adjust to the overwhelming effects of bulimia's rise. In my practice, I invite individuals to map their journey through this migration, recognising that their relationship with bulimia is neither singular nor linear but shaped by multiple movements – both chosen and imposed – that range from significant life transitions to momentary shifts. This mapping emphasises the fluidity of the journey, highlighting the interplay between personal transformation and bulimia's relentless changes. In doing so, despair is reconceptualised not as an endpoint, but as part of a complex, spiralling process of moving from how things are to how they might be – from *being* to *becoming*.

An externalising understanding (on the therapist's part) is foundational for receiving and responding to these experiences of despair and displacement. Yet, I have noticed that externalising questions that focus on the immediate effects of bulimia's wave can intensify scrutiny of a person's relationship with food, the body and health. Pathologising biomedical discourses, particularly in the context of neoliberal mental health services, often invite individualised notions of self-care. The urgency to "amend" can also subtly enter the conversation, bringing self-blame and shame into the room. Suddenly, it feels too crowded!

In my own experience of receiving therapy, I recall that questions such as "What has bulimia tried to convince you of?" or "How have you resisted bulimia?" – while theoretically grounded – had unexpected effects. It felt as though my timing and the therapist's were out of sync. While I was still grappling with the shock of bulimia's sudden rise and its embodied effects in the present moment, such questions felt like a push to take a position before I had made sense of how I had arrived in the conversation. This unintentionally created a divide, leaving me torn between aligning with the therapist or with bulimia. When those sorts of questions were asked, bulimia watched me closely on one side, the therapist stood on the other. In those moments, it felt far less risky – though no less painful – to align with bulimia. Quietly, I would turn away from the therapist, so subtly that they might not even notice, as I charted a course through the conversation that kept bulimia from feeling alienated. In doing so, the connection with the therapist would strain almost imperceptibly until it eventually frayed, and I was left alone once again, with only bulimia.

The women I have worked with have taught me that jumping into the statement of position maps during bulimia's rising tides is like stepping on to a tightrope without checking the safety net first. Without full permission and a thoughtful approach, our co-research risks replicating the very power relations we aim to challenge. Informed by the effects of my practice and what people shared with me, I began to reflect on what adjustments to narrative practice might be needed to better fit the particular context of work with bulimia. What new possibilities might arise from adaptations in navigating bulimia crises or feelings of entrapment within one's own body?

My approach to narrative practice maintains that the theoretical approach and direct practice need to be conceptualised in relation to each other. The most meaningful moments of co-research in my own experience of receiving narrative therapy were those that created space to contextualise bulimia's recent tides.

Michael White encouraged us to situate problems within broader cultural contexts such as race, gender and class (M. White, 2007). These conversations helped me to notice how gender expectations and medicalised discourses were shaping my own life, and to consider actions that could reclaim territories that had been taken away from me. In my practice, women have also taught me that while bulimia is often described as the outcome of such structural pressures and injustices, it can sometimes be experienced as something more: a response to the ways these contextual forces are lived out in immediate contexts and relationships – for example, through family pressures, intimate partnerships, or experiences of displacement from safety, identity or rights.

Attending in this way has profoundly influenced how I join with others in conversation. Rather than focusing solely on mapping bulimia's effects and unpacking the contexts in which it has taken hold, I have learnt to pause and wonder, together with the person, what the tides might be responding to in the particular circumstances of their life, and what this understanding might make possible for them to discern.

Women have also shown me that alongside the force of bulimia's tides there are small, careful and creative ways they find to endure and move through them. These can be understood as acts of survival. At the same time, I have noticed a risk in framing bulimia only as an enemy or an invading force. When conversations settle into this single-storied view, they can inadvertently reproduce a battle-like orientation that leaves little space to notice what else bulimia might be speaking of. An alternative possibility I have been drawn to consider, shaped by these conversations, is whether bulimia itself might sometimes be understood as a form of testimony: a turbulent expression of protest or witness to what has been unjust, violated or silenced. Through conversations with women, I have explored attending to what is "absent but implicit" in bulimia's tides within the intersecting contexts of their lives. I have noticed that this way of working can open space for multiple understandings to emerge, such as viewing these tides as possible protests against oppression or trauma.

When engaging with what is absent but implicit in people's experiences of bulimia's tides, we can focus on determining which aspects of a person's experience to highlight amidst intersecting oppression. This approach, shaped by my work with women across diverse contexts, is demonstrated the following section in which I draw on an example from the overlapping practice areas of trauma/abuse and bulimia.

Story of practice Bulimia's rise as a testimony or protest

My work with Maria, a woman navigating bulimia, has deeply shaped my approach to working with the absent but implicit in response to bulimia's turbulent tides. One session stands out. Maria described feeling like the "snake" – her name for bulimia – had swallowed her whole. In previous sessions, we externalised the snake, placed it in context, and explored the steps Maria had already taken to avoid its venom, recognising her skills and values (M. White, 2007). Although I thought we were really hitting our stride, then came the curveball! I checked in with Maria about her experience of the conversation so far. I am deeply grateful for her honesty – she expressed her frustration, catching me completely by surprise.

The snake, always lurking, had been striking with its "poisoned bites" more often lately, leaving her wanting to hide from her own body. She explained that our externalising conversations felt like an unwelcome magnifying glass on the snake that reinforced the urgency to "do something" while she was still grappling with the shock of its recent bites. Reflecting on this had me wondering whether it was the deconstruction part of externalising or asking Maria to take a position or something else that felt overwhelming. This reconnected me to my own experience: the more the therapy I was receiving focused on bulimia during times of raising tides, the more it seemed to puff up its chest and thrive on that attention, almost as if it got bolder the more we talked about it. This was when I felt a need to shift my approach, moving beyond externalising conversations to something more expansive, where attention could be given to the nuances of Maria's experience, without reinforcing the feeling that bulimia was the dominant force in the room.

I asked Maria about the direction she'd prefer for our conversation, but she expressed uncertainty, mentioning that she had assumed the session "should" focus on her bulimic episodes. This tension underscores the importance of maintaining a co-research stance (Epston, 1999; Epston & White, 1992; M. White, 1995) and resisting the idea that narrative therapy can be "rolled out" as a series of maps. What might initially seem like a dead end in conversation can, instead, become an opportunity to explore the very process of the co-research itself.

Instead of pushing the conversation forward, we slowed down to "loiter with intent" (Epston, 1999) around Maria's experienced location within the conversation. I asked Maria, "As you mention that focusing on the bites of the snake isn't helpful today, what do you notice? What's it like to bring that into our shared space? What emerges for you in this particular moment?" By staying with how people arrive in the present moment, we can always find potential avenues for co-research (Braidotti, 2006).

Bringing the focus back to the present ensures accountability to co-research by positioning both of us as active, collaborative participants moving "from the known and familiar to what is possible to know" (M. White, 2007, p. 263), rather than making decisions in isolation. In this context, slowing down was an intentional and politically significant practice, as this shift in pace disrupted the pressure for immediate action – a crucial stance, especially when healing from the aftermath of bulimia's tide might require time and special care.

Shifting our focus away from the snake allowed other aspects of Maria's life to come forward. She shared that the snake had been present throughout the abusive relationship she was enduring, but it became even more prominent whenever she prepared or attempted to leave. I asked, "What was happening in your life in the months leading up to your decision to leave the relationship? Who has been alongside you during these hard times?" Maria said that no-one was aware of her experience of abuse, and this often invited feelings of despair and isolation. We discussed Maria's experience of this despair and isolation, and how they manifested in her life. We talked about the contexts of this despair, which included socioeconomic conditions that kept her entrapped in the abusive relationship and silenced her voice. This had me interested in what was absent but implicit in Maria's despair. I asked, "When you speak about the despair of being silenced in the abuse, is there anything that you feel is important to have witnessed, to be acknowledged in your decision to leave?" Maria expressed that having "no-one knowing" seemed to disqualify her survival skills and knowledges. She wished to be seen for what she had endured and acknowledged for what it takes to leave. She also wished she didn't have to make risky life-changing decisions on her own.

Vikki Reynolds (2013, p. 33) pointed out that women's trauma is often framed as a medical issue rather than a systemic one. In the conversations

I am part of, connections between trauma and bulimia frequently emerge, reflecting broader systemic forces at play. Given that bulimic episodes increased as Maria prepared to leave the relationship, I grew curious about the role the snake played in her experience of living in silence. I asked, "Was the snake present in moments of fear? Has it witnessed the oppressive practices and attitudes you faced?" In this way, the snake – as a metaphor for bulimia – was repositioned not only as a force of disruption but also as a witness to Maria's struggles. Maria confirmed that the snake had indeed been present, seeing her through experiences of violence and threat and deeply aware of what it means to survive those moments of despair. Positioning the snake in this way created space for Maria to consider that its presence might not only bring harm, but also speak of her endurance and her refusal to remain silent in the face of violence. I have since found that this repositioning, from adversary to witness, can also open possibilities in other conversations where women describe living with both trauma and bulimia.

Since no-one else knew about her experiences of abuse, I asked Maria what it meant for her to have a witness to her survival skills in moments of fear and uncertainty, even if that witness was non-corporeal – such as the snake in this case. I then wondered aloud, "If I asked the snake directly, what might it testify about your experience of violence? What aspects of your being have been violated, and which beliefs or values have been transgressed by ongoing oppression?" Reynolds (2013) suggested that what is often labelled as "depression" might be more accurately understood as "oppression". This perspective helped bridge gaps in my work with Maria, resonating with the feminist view that personal issues frequently have political roots (Hanisch, 1969).

I deliberately maintained the focus of my questions on the immediate context of violence, rather than retracing the history of bulimia in Maria's life. When we meet with people facing the aftermath of bulimia's turbulent tides, it is not always necessary to engage in a full unpacking of the person's history with bulimia or a broader deconstruction of bulimia. Instead, focusing on the present creates space for response-based practice, without delving into multiple timescapes unless this becomes relevant or warranted.

Maria described how the snake seemed to resist the invisibility of the oppression it had witnessed. The snake refused to remain silent about the violence Maria had endured. This refreshed understanding began to loosen the totality of bulimia's domination. From here, we could ask further questions: if the snake was acting in protest, what exactly was it protesting against? And, equally, what might it have been protesting *for*? These reflections opened space for Maria to begin seeing the snake not only as a witness but also as participating in her protest against the violence and control she had suffered. In this light, the snake could be seen as a testament to what had been precious to Maria and violated (M. White, 2003).

Although the snake brought Maria frustration and despair, Maria noticed that, within the high-risk context of the abusive relationship, the snake often held a position of power that she herself could not safely access. While Maria was working "in the shadows" to escape violence, the snake seemed to embody a protest that Maria, for safety's sake, could not yet express fully and openly. I was deeply moved when Maria described looking at herself in the mirror, noticing the physical effects of a recent bulimic episode, such as weight gain, and feeling as if she could actually hear the snake within her body crying out against the violence: "enough is enough!" We explored how sitting with bulimia's impact on her body – at least for a while – could be understood as a physical statement of position: a stance against gender oppression.

In unpacking with Maria what bulimia exists in the face of, I found thinking about the absent but implicit particularly relevant. Together, we explored how she was able to discern what bulimia might be advocating for, even amid feelings of frustration and despair. Maria noted that she understood a bit about advocacy. She recalled her dear cousin whom she often witnessed showing solidarity and care through activist work. I asked Maria what the snake's form of advocacy might signify about what Maria was departing from in her relationship and where she hoped to go. This led us into the realm of what is precious, treasured and even sacred. Maria identified care, safety, integrity and solidarity as her preferred values, and we examined her knowledge of fostering community. This co-research led us to trace the social and relational history of her community-building skills, moving further into rich story development in relation to her hopes, commitments and life purposes.

I invited Maria to consider whether the snake that had advocated for relationships of care, safety and solidarity on her behalf against oppression might step back temporarily, allowing us to explore her current resistances alongside others or consider possible collective or community steps. This approach avoided an assumption of opposition or animosity between the person and bulimia, opening space for nuanced exploration of their relationship(s).

Together, we drew on Maria's community-building skills to explore how they might support her in gathering a support network around her. We took considerable time to craft a safety plan for exiting the relationship, engaging a group of trusted people to avoid further harm. Throughout this preparation, Maria moved cautiously, operating under the radar of control and navigating through a fog of fear and uncertainty. Resistance is not solely about direct confrontation; it can also involve subtler, strategic actions and decisions (Wade, 2007). Together we explored how Maria's silence was not simply an effect of fear but an intentional act of self-protection that reflected her personal agency.

In our discussions, it became clear that Maria's experience was part of a broader narrative shared by many women facing violence (Pederson, 2024). Feminist narrative practices encouraged us to promote solidarity rather than individualise her struggle (Kitzinger & Perkins, 1993). I gently enquired about whether Maria might be interested in joining a group that I was facilitating, and she agreed. The group, made up of women who had escaped abusive relationships, offered invaluable collective solidarity. As bell hooks (1984) emphasised, collective care is essential for resisting oppression and fostering healing. Our group work included narrative documentation and sharing these stories with others, supporting the women to "speak through me" to others (Denborough, 2008). A detailed account of this approach is beyond the scope of this paper.

From practice to broader reflections

Contemporary understandings of bulimia often obscure the complexities and particularities of its tides, drawing a "natural" and linear link between bulimia and distress. This can lead therapeutic conversations to focus primarily on the most visible aspects of bulimia's operations. When therapy emphasises lengthy exploration of bulimia as the main character in the room, even when using externalising language, people can become immersed in its tides. Bulimia is often framed as "the main problem", and the distress accompanying its different tides is viewed as a natural outcome of bulimia's long history in the person's life.

This naturalistic account dismisses the particularities of the varied and shifting contexts in which these tides emerge and recede over time, leaving people with an unsettling sense that the edges of their being are constantly at risk of being crossed in ways that are unpredictable or out of control. It also tends to replicate dualistic thinking, which risks constructing a fragile or vulnerable sense of self. For example, naturalistic accounts of bulimia are frequently shaped by an enemy/victim dualism.

When people describe their experience of bulimia's tides, I invite them to identify the contexts in which these tides emerged. This unpacking allows for alternative understandings of bulimia that take in complexities and particularities. When sharing what bulimia's tides are in relation to, people may voice concerns, laments, complaints, frustration, disappointment, distress, confusion or despair about specific situations in their lives. These can be seen as actions that bulimia embodies through its tides. I listen for places where I can ask questions that help people to characterise the forces they are up against in an externalised form. For example, I might ask:

- What are you protesting or lamenting here that bulimia seems to know about?

- What is happening in your life that you are refusing to go along with, and in this refusal, what is bulimia speaking up for?

- As you question what has been going on in your life, what might bulimia be inviting you to reclaim?

- Is bulimia aware of the ways you are challenging what has been done to you or others?

People's expressions might be named as actions, such as an objection, refusal, protest or questioning, emphasising personal agency. Similarly, the expression of bulimia's tides can be understood as refusal to relinquish what was so powerfully disrespected, and explorations of people's skills in maintaining a relationship with these intentional states can be very significantly elevating of their sense of who they are and of what their lives are about. In my practice, people have shared how bulimia's tides can act as reminders or wake-up calls, pointing to areas in their lives that may need to be attended to or reviewed. They often count this as a position in relation to bulimia's rise. Questions about the absent but implicit can help to identify where the person stands in terms of their personal experience with bulimia. If we view bulimia's tides as a testament to what a person holds precious –

what might have been compromised or violated through hardship – then the experienced intensity of bulimia's operations can be considered to be a reflection of the degree to which these intentional states were held precious. These implicit accounts are a rich source of material for preferred stories.

This approach does not seek to romanticise bulimia, nor to minimise or obscure its intrusive and often long-lasting harmful effects. The impact of traumatic or oppressive environments produces the coexistence of creative means of responding or protesting that may be simultaneously harmful or helpful in the long term. Thus, experiences of safety, control, fear, power and identity are critical in this work. As feminist narrative therapists, we can double listen to stories, attuning to the absent but implicit in order to uncover more nuanced understandings of bulimia's roles and operations during difficult times, as well as the shifting, multifaceted relationship(s) a person develops with bulimia in response to life's challenges.

The questions we ask and those we choose not to ask

Reflecting on the medicalisation of my experiences, I've come to appreciate that we are accountable not only for the questions we ask but also for those we choose not to ask. In my work with people dealing with bulimia, I intentionally resist asking questions about weight, food management or body metrics that might replicate clinical descriptions and evoke experiences of failure. Narrative therapy, after all, centres deconstruction, power, context, intersectionality and safety (Anderson, 1997).

Storytelling and listening are often messy, nuanced and political. Considering the intentions behind questioning, I recognise that the questions we ask – or choose not to ask – have political implications. They signal which stories we, as active witnesses, are prepared and willing to receive and which conversations or discourses we deliberately resist participating in. At times, this awareness reveals a shift from what "should" be told to what it is possible to tell. This challenges the dominant idea that therapists should be "neutral". I find this understanding particularly helpful in turning my curiosities into questions that are response-based, deconstructive, invitational, political and relational – moving from problem-solving, management and saving to positioning myself as co-researcher.

Influence of lived experience on practice

Lived experiences can greatly influence how we come to our practices, creating a relational collaboration that extends beyond traditional mental health systems and ethics. People often seek me out after watching my videos, wandering my website, glimpsing me on TV or joining my workshops. By the time they reach me, they sometimes know parts of my story better than I do! I'm publicly open about my lived experience with bulimia. This kind of transparency often enables me to join in the conversation from a solid ground of shared experiences, where insider knowledges meet curiosity, and resonance encourages two-way transport. I deeply value this collective space of "mutual contributions" (M. White, 1997). Establishing a strong therapeutic alliance with an "ethic of care and collaboration" (M. White, 1997) is a vital component of trauma work, particularly with individuals labelled as "bulimic", who often, and understandably, grapple with fear of judgement and the imposition of external meanings and power over our lived experiences. The term "solidarity conversations" frequently pops up in feedback from those I engage with in therapeutic conversations, reflecting a kind of co-research that isn't typically found in clinical settings. I couldn't describe it better than Maria, who said that our time together often felt like I was swimming alongside her while she weathered the tide. As she traversed the currents beneath the surface, it felt as though we extended our hands to one another, finding balance in the waves together, rather than her struggling alone.

Engaging with people's stories often reconnects me with my own insider knowledge, yet this requires careful navigation of my power and privilege. It is crucial to reflect on how our lived experiences shape our assumptions and influence the questions we ask or don't ask. Making these assumptions visible for scrutiny is an essential part of accountability. I may offer a summary or editorial using the person's own words, articulating how their expressions resonate with my experiences. Then, I check to see if my insights align with theirs. If not, we explore together how recognising this difference might shape their understandings of their own experience. At times, my insider knowledge shapes my curiosity and highlights particular elements in people's descriptions. Rather than immediately offering a question, I remain transparent about this influence and seek permission before introducing the question. This practice underscores the complexity of staying decentred while drawing from my own lived experience.

I also like to ponder how my lived experience with bulimia shapes my practice in contrast to practitioners of different genders who might be missing that particular flavour. I wonder if different vantage points might keep certain power relations in play, like a sneaky puppeteer pulling strings behind the scenes. I'd love to hear from others about what unique considerations might be needed for practitioners of diverse genders and how their approaches might differ from mine.

Final words

The journey of writing this paper has been both challenging and therapeutic, as it weaves together not only my practice but also my lived experience. Throughout this process, bulimia has made its presence felt in complex ways, responding persistently to the act of writing. At times, it felt like an ongoing conversation – bulimia asserting itself while I wrote and me, in turn, writing back. The process was not just about documenting my experience but also about reclaiming space, carving out a place where I could speak about my ongoing, ever-shifting relationship with bulimia rather than it speaking for me. Writing became both an act of resistance and an offering – a testimony of solidarity shaped by the conversations, feedback and shared reflections of those who engaged with this work. This piece now stands as something I can touch, read and return to, a marker of the movements between myself and bulimia, where I no longer find myself pulled under by its currents but instead move with the tides, learning when to stand firm and when to flow.

In many ways, this act of writing connects to the solidarity I have experienced in therapeutic and community spaces where stories are held, voices are amplified and no-one is left to navigate alone. I hope this paper makes a meaningful contribution to the conversation on bulimia and resonates with practitioners, people dealing with bulimia, families, friends and others. The concept of solidarity conversations, as shared by the women I work with, aligns with the kind of therapeutic co-research I aspire to engage in. I find Poh Lee Lin's words deeply moving: "If I have access to power in a moment when you might have less access, I will meet you in those moments rather than watch you flounder – as others have done for me at different moments in this intentional engagement with power through communal practice" (P. L. Lee, personal communication, November, 2023). Reflecting on my own experiences, I've been profoundly supported by those who have stood by me through challenging times. This form of solidarity – leveraging community resources to support one another – is at the heart of my practice. This paper embodies my commitment to politically include my lived experience as an act of solidarity with the community of narrative practitioners and, most importantly, with those of us navigating complex relationships with bulimia. My intention is not to overshadow or dominate but to meet readers in the gaps, fostering a collaborative reflection on how we practice and move forward together.

Acknowledgments

This paper may never have been written without the encouragement of Peter Hollams and Meredith Oliver, whose casual coffee conversation planted the seed for this work. They reminded me that perhaps what I've been through carries value – not just for me but for others, too.

I am deeply grateful to Poh Lin Lee, whose unwavering support, mentorship and friendship have been pivotal. From mentally preparing me to begin writing, to co-producing the insider knowledges that shape the ethics, positioning and ideas within these pages, her presence has been a constant source of encouragement and inspiration.

I extend heartfelt thanks to Kristina Lainson, Poh Lee Lin, Natalia Tounta and Adam Charvatis for reading drafts, offering thoughtful feedback, and challenging me to expand my thinking. I am also indebted to Cheryl White and David Denborough for their ongoing encouragement and support.

Finally, I wish to express my profound gratitude to the people I work with in therapeutic conversations, especially Maria. Their courage in sharing parts of their stories and journeys has profoundly informed and enriched the ideas explored in this paper.

Notes

1 Including my own experience of receiving narrative therapy is an intentional and political choice to make visible how lived experience directly shapes my practice. This challenges traditional hierarchies that privilege clinical or academic expertise over insider knowledge, and instead asserts lived experience as a legitimate and valuable source of insight, equally – if not more – vital in therapeutic work.

2 In Greek, the word "bulimia" is gendered as she/her, carrying specific implications. From my extensive experience working with individuals affected by bulimia, I have noticed that when bulimia is personified using she/her, it often leads to assumptions about its "personality". Pronouns such as she/her and he/him are tied to broader cultural notions of gender. I recognise that these pronouns may not resonate with everyone across different contexts and languages. Therefore, in this paper, I use "it" to invite diversity and encourage readers to reflect on how they might support individuals in naming their experience of bulimia using their own preferred words and pronouns, if any.

3 Performativity of gender is a stylised repetition of acts, an imitation or miming of the dominant conventions of gender.

4 Although bulimia is experienced by people across genders, this paper focuses specifically on women's experiences, as these have shaped both my own lived experience and my therapeutic practice. I acknowledge that experiences of bulimia may be different for people situated in other gendered positions.

References

Anderson, H. (1997). *Conversation, language, and possibilities: A postmodern approach to therapy.* Basic Books.

Braidotti, R. (2006). *Transpositions: On nomadic ethics.* Polity.

Butler, J. (1990). *Gender trouble: Feminism and the subversion of identity.* Routledge.

Crawford, R. (1980). Healthism and the medicalization of everyday life. *International Journal of Health Services, 10*(3), 365–388. https://doi.org/10.2190/3h2h-3xjn-3kay-g9ny

Denborough, D. (2008). *Collective narrative practice: Responding to individuals, groups and communities who have experienced trauma.* Dulwich Centre Publications.

Epston, D. (1999). Co-research: The making of an alternative knowledge. *Dulwich Centre Journal,* (2), 21–28.

Epston, D., Morris, F., & Maisel, R. (1995). *Biting the hand that starves you: Inspiring resistance to anorexia/bulimia.* Norton.

Epston, D., & White, M. (1992). *Experience, contradiction, narrative and imagination.* Dulwich Centre Publications.

Foucault, M. (1973). *The birth of the clinic: An archaeology of medical perception.* Pantheon.

Hamann, T. H. (2009). Neoliberalism, governmentality, and ethics. *Foucault Studies, 6,* 37–59. https://doi.org/10.22439/fs.v0i0.2471

Hanisch, C. (1969). The personal is political. In S. Firestone & A. Koedt (Eds.), *Notes from the second year: Women's liberation, major writings of the radical feminists* (pp. 76–78). Radical Feminism.

Hegarty, K., Smith, K., & Hegarty, L. (2010). Applying narrative therapy to the care of women who have experienced domestic violence. *Australian Family Physician, 39*(6), 410–413.

hooks, b. (1984). *Feminist theory: From margin to center.* South End Press.

Kitzinger, C., & Perkins, R. (1993). *Changing our minds: Lesbian feminism and psychology.* New York University Press.

Lainson, K. (2016). From "disorder" to political action: Conversations that invite collective considerations to individual experiences of women who express concerns about eating and their bodies. *International Journal of Narrative Therapy and Community Work,* (2), 1–12.

Maisel, R., Epston, D., & Borden, A. (2004). *Biting the hand that starves you: Inspiring resistance to anorexia/bulimia.* Norton.

Madigan, S., & Epston, D. (1995). From "spy-chiatric" gaze to communities of concern: From professional monologue to dialogue. In S. Friedman (Ed.), *The reflecting team in action: Collaborative practice in family therapy* (pp. 257–276). Guilford.

Pedersen, K. (2016). Uncovering bulimia's demanding voice: Challenges from a narrative therapist's perspective. *Dulwich Centre Journal,* (4), 1–12.

Pederson, L. (2024). *Honouring resistance and building solidarity: Feminism and narrative practice.* Dulwich Centre Publications.

Reynolds, V. (2013). *Justice-doing at the intersections of power.* Dulwich Centre Publications.

Turner, V. (1969). *The ritual process.* Cornell University Press.

van Gennep, A. (1960). *The rites of passage.* University of Chicago Press. (Original work published 1909)

Wade, A. (2007). Small acts of living: Everyday resistance to violence and other forms of oppression. *Journal of Family Violence, 22*(7), 489–492.

White, C., & Hales, J. (Eds.). (1997). *The personal is the professional: Therapists reflect on their families, lives and work*. Dulwich Centre Publications.

White, M. (1995). Therapeutic documents revisited. In M White (Ed.), *Re-authoring lives: Interviews and essays* (pp. 199–213). Dulwich Centre Publications.

White, M. (1997). *Narratives of therapists' lives*. Dulwich Centre Publications.

White, M. (2000). *Reflections on narrative practice: Essays and interviews*. Dulwich Centre Publications.

White, M. (2003). Narrative practice and community assignments. *International Journal of Narrative Therapy and Community Work*, (2), 17–55.

White, M. (2007). *Maps of narrative practice*. Norton.

White, M. (2011). *Narrative practice: Continuing the conversations*. Norton.

White, M., & Epston, D. (1990). *Narrative means to therapeutic ends*. Norton.

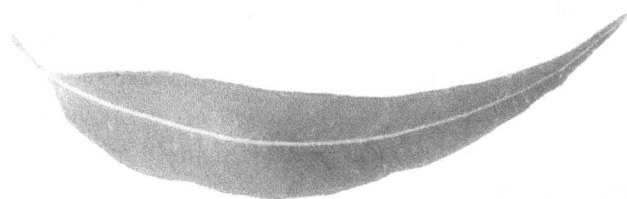

"Pockets of freedom":

Creating therapeutic spaces as refuges for Black experiences of neurodivergence

by Sandra Coral

Sandra Coral is an integrative narrative and somatic practitioner, former specialist teacher (gifted education and other additional learning needs) and writer who predominantly works with neurodivergent people from multiply marginalised identity groups, empowering them to recover their unique ways to thrive while still navigating the daily pressures of living under systems of oppression. She also supports workplaces and schools in becoming more neurodiversity affirming, trauma-informed and equity-centred environments. Their podcast and Substack newsletter, Neurodivergent Narratives, *centres the unique challenges, perspectives and experiences of neurodivergence and healing for historically excluded communities. Sandra is also a new author, having published* It's Never Just ADHD: Finding the child behind the label *(Sage) in 2024. Sandra is a Canadian living in England with her partner and their child.* sandra@ndnarratives.com

ORCID ID: https://orcid.org/0009-0007-9071-876X

Abstract

The influence of Eurocentricism on therapy spaces makes them unsafe for Black people. This is compounded for Black people whose lives are impacted by their neurodivergence, and therapeutic support needs to account for that. This paper demonstrates how integrating the tenets of critical race theory alongside narrative practice can guide therapists and others in helping professions in creating what Makungu Akinyela has called "pockets of freedom". These are therapeutic environments free from the interpretations and judgements of the dominant culture, and which serve as a refuge for Black people (with neurodivergence) to heal from the effects of colonialism.

Key words: neurodivergence; neuronormativity; gifted; race; racism; Black people; critical race theory; whiteness; intersectionality; narrative therapy; narrative practice

Coral, S. (2025). "Pockets of Freedom": Creating therapeutic spaces as refuges for Black experiences of neurodivergence. *International Journal of Narrative Therapy and Community Work*, (2), 61–72. https://doi.org/10.4320/EJDR6304

Author pronouns: she/they

In my first meeting with Michael, a Black man in his early 30s, he described feeling disconnected and isolated. He attributed this disheartening state to his extremely high intelligence, seeing it as something that set him apart from others, including in the Black community. While growing up, Michael had dealt with the impact of gang life and police brutality around him. When he was a child in school, people in positions of power viewed him as a threat, not only because of his intelligence but, more significantly, because he dared to be so intelligent while being Black. To meet his learning needs, it was suggested that Michael skip three grade levels, but his mother felt that this could be detrimental to his emotional and social development. With no offers to address his mother's concerns, his school ultimately did nothing, leaving Michael to fend for himself. His incredible knowledges, unique perspectives and the skills his intelligence produced were rarely acknowledged. He grew to dislike himself because of the problems his intelligence created. His high intelligence alienated him from the Black community, but despite his intelligence, because he was Black he wasn't accepted by the dominant culture either.

Intersectionality and neurodiversity

The term Intersectionality was coined by Kimberlé Crenshaw (1989). She recognised that Black women's experiences of discrimination were missing from both feminist and anti-racist theory because their single-dimensional analyses of discrimination "erased Black women in the conceptualisation, identification and remediation of race and gender discrimination by limiting the inquiry to the experiences of otherwise-privileged members of the group" (1989, p. 140), such as white women and Black men. Crenshaw developed intersectional analysis to centre the particular experiences of people for whom "Black" and "woman" constituted one distinct identity rather than two separate and discrete experiences. Intersectionality made visible the problematic consequences of viewing racial and gender discrimination separately, and it can also be applied to the compounding experiences of those who are both Black and neurodivergent.

Nick Walker (2021, p. 26) defined neurodiversity as "the diversity of human minds, the infinite variation of neurocognitive functioning within our species". Within this diversity, normative ways of accessing, processing and communicating information are defined as "neurotypical". The idea of a "typical" brain is a social construct, much like race and gender, not an actually

existing neurotype. It's also important to note that the Eurocentricity of notions of neuronormativity informs a focus on professionalism, the prioritisation of the written word over oral knowledge, ways education is organised and learning is assessed, what knowledge and skills are considered valuable, and whose ideas and experiences are centred in that knowledge (Jones & Okun, 2001; Okun, 2021). Any experiences that are seen to deviate from this normative construct, including ADHD, Tourette syndrome, obsessive compulsive disorder, autism, psychosis or traumatic brain injury, can be considered forms of neurodivergence.[1] Extremely high intelligence may also be seen as neurodivergent, partly because of its impact on a person's social, emotional and sensory needs.

The more closely a person can *generally* adhere to and function under the expectations of the dominant culture, the more power they can *usually* access in society. People whose neurotypes diverge from social norms are not as readily accepted by many in society, and are not adequately accommodated in schools and workplaces. This can lead to them being shamed, blamed and unappreciated for the perspectives, knowledges and talents they possess. They often grow up traumatised from their school experiences, burnt out from trying to hide or change any signs of neurodivergence so they can better "fit in" with expectations at school or work, face mental health challenges like anxiety or depression, isolate due to social or communication differences (Coral, 2024), or struggle to find sustainable employment options as adults. But even after understanding all these challenges (and more), without utilising intersectionality, you'd *still* be erasing the specific experiences of ableism that marginalised groups encounter.

For example, extremely high intelligence is often considered an advantage by the dominant culture, especially when used in ways that are seen to benefit society. But it's also disproportionately noticed in children who are white.[2] Intelligence testing has its origins in eugenics, and has been used as "scientific" proof that people who are white (particularly those of higher economic status) are of superior intelligence. Standardised tests are used to "measure cultural conditioning and learned scholastic aptitude (as opposed to innate intelligence) … The poor and otherwise socially disadvantaged score lower, and data, aggregated by race and class, are used to promote the interests of the ruling elite" (Reddy, 2008, p. 673). Without considering these facts *and* the reasons for them, Michael's particular experiences of high intelligence as a *Black child* wouldn't be seen. Any assumptions made about his ability to receive adequate learning support or acknowledgment of his abilities would come from the single-dimensional lens of high intelligence as defined in relation to the most privileged groups in society. This lens wasn't helpful for Michael as a child, and surely wouldn't be helpful within the therapeutic spaces where he sought help as an adult.

Looking at neurodivergence through an intersectional lens requires therapists, counsellors and other neurodiversity-affirming helpers to reflect on our beliefs about neurodivergence, privilege, oppression and how power impacts a person's experience within society:

- What ways of thinking and processing information have I been taught to see as most valuable?

- How might I bring these beliefs and/or assumptions into the therapeutic space?

- How might presentations of neurodivergence be interpreted depending on what a person looks like, their race, gender expression, socioeconomic status?

- How might people around me interpret my ways of thinking, communicating and processing information based on my various social identities?

- When (if ever) have their interpretations accurately portrayed my experiences?

"Pockets of freedom"

Makungu Akinyela (2025, p. 15) drew on Frantz Fanon (1967) to describe the unique psychological experiences that impact a colonised person. Akinyela explained how surviving the dominant culture forces the colonised person to change themselves to become more aligned with Eurocentric norms. The hope is to be viewed as more human by the coloniser and, therefore, live more safely in society. But this behaviour alienates the colonised person from their communities. It creates *double consciousness*, in which different perspectives on a person's various social identities lead to difficulties in developing a sense of self. With this in mind, Michael and I aimed to co-create a preferred story of his neurodivergence, which included re-authoring his sense of self as a Black man, beyond the gaze of the dominant culture.

Most people consult me in a coaching capacity, expecting me to deliver solutions and the accountability necessary to accomplish them. However, it is important to take time for conversations about the realities of neurodivergence alongside lived experiences of social identities before moving to any goal-setting or problem-solving. This is especially true for those historically excluded from the social discourse that shapes the context of the problems that they consider to be keeping them from achieving their goals. Slowing down for conversation about the problem can reveal how the person has learnt to see themself, their experiences of neurodivergence, and their belief in their ability to meet their goals while navigating oppression. We can also recover the knowledges, beliefs, values and skills that have sustained them thus far. For people whose neurodivergence only adds to their further marginalisation in society, it is necessary to create therapeutic spaces where they feel safe enough to share their experiences.

Our work with those most marginalised must include creating what Akinyela has called "pockets of freedom". In a pocket of freedom, colonised people can "talk about their lives … make sense of their relationships, free from the interpretations and judgments of dominant Eurocentric culture" (2025, p. 16). This idea comes from the history of liberated spaces, including the histories of escaped societies of enslaved Africans who "created communities that became beacons of hope and liberation for those still enslaved". These were "liberated territories" where "people lived differently than they could in other spaces" (2025, p. 25).

> In some liberation movements, these liberated territories were specifically designated as places of healing for those involved in the ongoing struggle. These were places for people to go and rest and regather their energies before returning to the occupied territories to continue to struggle for freedom. (Akinyela, 2025, p. 25)

Akinyela has argued that critical African-centred theory is necessary for decolonising Africans' minds, bodies and spirits, suggesting "the need for Africans to develop a collective liberatory consciousness as a necessary act against Eurocentric control of Africans" (2025, p. 11). In this paper, I've chosen to situate Akinyela's ideas within a critical race theory (CRT) framework to reflect on the impact of colonisation on Black lives, including in therapeutic practices and spaces. CRT is more accessible to me as a transracial adoptee who grew up in rural Canada isolated from Black community. I explore how we might integrate a CRT perspective into creating our own safer therapeutic environments or "pockets of freedom" for Black people seeking therapy while considering their specific experiences of neurodivergence.

Critical race theory

The impacts of Eurocentrism on experiences of neurodiversity differ depending on a person's overlapping privileges and oppressions. However, being Black with neurodivergence is a distinct experience. Many spaces, including therapeutic ones, are inherently unsafe for Black people because people in positions of power (in this case, the therapist) define their experiences and then interpret their problems and possible solutions through a Eurocentric lens. Even with good intentions, therapists, educators and other neurodiversity-affirming helpers integrate dominant ideology into putatively "healing" or "safe" spaces. Doing so disempowers marginalised groups. It limits their potential for re-authoring stories by further disconnecting them from the knowledges and skills they've acquired from their own culture and experience. It keeps them from reclaiming a preferred identity, therefore reinforcing double consciousness.

Critical race theory acknowledges that racism is embedded in all the systems and structures of society, affecting the ways these structures work and who benefits from them. It "asks us to consider how we can transform the relationship between race, racism, and power and work towards the liberation of People of Colour" (Adaway, 2019). Black Lives Matter (n.d.) has imagined Black liberation as a world where "Black people across the diaspora thrive, experience joy, and are not defined by their struggles. In pursuing liberation, we envision a future fully divested from police, prisons, and all punishment paradigms and which invests in justice, joy, and culture".

Critical race theory is based on six tenets (Delgado & Stefancic, 2001):

1. racism as endemic: it's everywhere, from inside us to externally in our societal systems and throughout our daily lives

2. whiteness as property: everything has been created to benefit or support whiteness as the dominant culture

3. challenging historical narratives: the narratives of people from different races have changed over time, depending on how they benefit whiteness

4. intersectionality and anti-essentialism: there are many ways race impacts our lives that are unique to Black people

5. differential racialisation: racial justice/progress happens to the extent that there is something to benefit whiteness

6. voices of colour: those who experience racism are the best to speak on it.

Racism shapes Black people's experience of the systems and institutions of society. This also includes spaces perceived as "safe", such as a therapy room. The CRT framework could guide counsellors, teachers and other neurodiversity-affirming helpers in questioning and unlearning internalised biases they unwittingly bring into the healing space. Questions for reflection and discussion with others in your community on co-creating safer spaces could include:

- What narratives are you carrying about race (your own and others')?

- How are your beliefs about race benefiting the dominant culture?

- How are your beliefs about race challenging the ideology of the dominant culture?

- What parts of your culture and conditioning might you be bringing into the therapeutic space?

- How might your conditioning and social identity markers keep you from effectively co-creating a "pocket of freedom" with Black people?

- How can/are you use/using your position of power to co-create "pockets of freedom"?

The tenets of CRT describe the general experience of all Black people in a Eurocentric society. However, depending on additional overlapping oppressions and privileges, Black experiences are still incredibly diverse. Remember, not all oppressions impact a person's life equally, and Black people are not a monolith that's impacted uniformly. Intersectionality becomes an important tool to help "acknowledge that everyone has their own unique experiences of discrimination and oppression and we must consider everything and anything that can marginalise people" (Taylor, 2019). When we refuse to acknowledge how we benefit from the systems that oppress others, we'll never truly see the Other as human and deserving of the same opportunities to thrive. Creating pockets of freedom that truly feel like a refuge and healing space for Black people with neurodivergence[3] means continuously working to transform our relationship to race, neurodivergence and power, and how we use our power to support the liberation of all people.

Creating "pockets of freedom" through a critical race theory framework

I will show how I applied the six tenets of CRT in my work with Michael. I share extracts of our conversations, which took place both verbally and in writing. After each of our sessions together, Michael and I shared access to transcripts of our conversations. This enabled us to further engage with each other's words and ideas by adding additional thoughts, insights and questions to the text. Michael could reflect on and further externalise the problem, and I could uncover more unique outcomes to develop in later conversations.[4]

Racism as endemic

For Black, brown, Indigenous and other melanated people, racism is an everyday part of life. It's not just in how we interact with others but is also embedded in our institutions, systems and culture. It shapes how we see ourselves because racial trauma is internalised and embedded in our bodies, and everyday stressors, microaggressions and lack of regard add extra layers of challenges in all areas of our lives (Menakem, 2017). What's more, for Black and other colonised people, it's "never simply that we compare ourselves with other people, but that we judge ourselves and our relationships through Eurocentric norms and values" (Menakem, 2017, p. 160). This results in Black people alienating ourselves from our communities, our culture and ourselves in the hope of being safer and "fitting in" with the expectations of the dominant culture, but never truly feeling "good enough" or safe enough to be ourselves. For Michael, this meant trying to "escape the demands of The Blob" (his metaphor for white supremacist society) and how he was treated, which directly impacted the ways he learnt to see himself as a Black person and his neurodivergence. In conversation, Michael said:

> Okay, now this person [referring to himself] is a threat. And so ... it didn't take me long as a kid to figure out, like, "Okay, I'm not supposed to say these things. I'm not supposed to ask these questions. They can't help me". And not only that, they're going to be spiteful about it.

In the transcript of this conversation, the following written dialogue took place.

Sandra: I'm just thinking here about the fact that you felt like you would be a threat to the adults around you for asking questions – that moving you to a higher grade was more about their needs than yours. Was this when you first realised that people weren't really seeing you, but you saw their motives? It's such an interesting word to use, "threat", like this kid is a danger. I'm wondering what a kid might learn to think about themselves when they believe that they're a threat at such a young age.

Michael: Yeah, pretty much. Getting in trouble like getting sent to the office every week or every other week for minor things, getting bullied by other kids and teachers essentially turning the other way because I was already "difficult", getting hit with a belt by my dad FOR [Michael capitalised this] getting in trouble all the time. Asking too many questions people couldn't answer and their nasty responses, getting berated for having "good parents" and so having no reason to "act out" – things of that nature. Sustained over time, pretty much the majority of my early school time. Let alone pop culture and the media I would consume on my own that made it clear Blackness, when not fetishised or entertaining, is something not wanted or appreciated, often feared. When I got older and had more interactions with law enforcement and bigger institutions and forces, it became increasingly clear. And scary.

Sandra: Where does one go, what does one do, when no-one within the spaces they're dependent on sees them?

Michael: I think we just learn to adapt, which to me was just creating space, even if I had to fight for it.

Black people are closely monitored (or policed) in schools and workplaces, which makes us vigilant about our surroundings and how we're behaving in them. We grow up enduring harsher punishments in school than other students (particularly those who are white) for the same "offences". But as Black people with neurodivergence, we become even more hypervigilant about how we're perceived at work, at school and in the wider world. We endured the same type of treatment as other Black children, but our presentations of neurodivergence were interpreted as aggressiveness, defiance, laziness or unintelligence (Coral, 2024). We learnt that we must change ourselves by hiding any expressions of neurodivergence in our communication, thinking or work styles. But this isn't easily accomplished or sustainable without heavy costs to our self-esteem and wellbeing. It's also made more difficult when considering that those same characteristics of neurodivergence are imposed on *all* Black people by the dominant culture simply because we're Black. No matter how hard we try, no matter what we do or don't do, we can't escape them. This is also true when we're in "healing" or "safe" spaces that are deeply influenced by Eurocentric ideals.

Black people often come into therapeutic spaces with problem stories ingrained in them from the dominant culture. Therapists and other neurodiversity-affirming helpers must be committed to continually learning to identify and interrogate Eurocentric beliefs that may influence not only their beliefs and therapeutic practices, but also those of the Black people who come to work with them. "Oppressed people often internalise the trauma-based values and strategies of their oppressors. These values and strategies need to be consciously noticed … and challenged" (Menakem, 2017, p. 79). Narrative therapy understands that "problems are located outside of persons", which makes "it more likely that matters of gender, class, culture, race, sexuality and ability are considered in therapeutic conversations" (Hammoud-Beckett, 2007, p. 113). We can define the problem within a context that is closer to the person's experience. This also allows us "to name and acknowledge broader relations of power and instances of injustice that have contributed to the problem" (Russell & Carey, 2004, p. 118). Identity is contextual and relational, not fixed. We must ask questions that encourage Black people to explore their relationships with the different identities represented in the problem story, to support the re-authoring of their preferred story. This includes asking questions about neurodivergence.

Whiteness as property

Critical race theory encourages us to remember that claims about colour blindness and meritocracy will never be true because when race and racism are integrated throughout society, it's not possible to be neutral about them. Suggesting this enables the dominant culture to take no responsibility for ending the oppression of Black, brown, Indigenous and other melanated people. It also hides how whiteness works to maintain its power. This tenet of CRT aligns with Akinyela's (2025) suggestion that part of our job in

creating "pockets of freedom" is being "consciously aware of the ways in which the dominant Eurocentric culture can influence the lives of New Afrikan people and in creating a context in which families can come to their understandings about their lives" (p. 20). Narrative therapy gives us tools to challenge dominant ideology by questioning subjugating discourses that support people's dominant and unhelpful stories. This allows us to make visible the dominant culture's influence on people's lives.

Foucault used the term "games of truth" to describe "a set of rules by which truth is produced" (1997, p. 297). As Black people with neurodivergence, we face many different "truths" at once. Externalising the problems in a person's life can help to make visible the discourses and truth claims that contribute to them, making them available for analysis. Exposing the sociopolitical practices that create such truths opens space to discover other ways of understanding our experience, including understandings that could better support us to create change. Delgado and Stefancic (2001) suggested that

> Stories can name a type of discrimination (e.g., microaggressions, unconscious discrimination, or structural racism); once named, it can be combated. If race is not real or objective but constructed, racism and prejudice should be capable of deconstruction; the pernicious beliefs and categories are, after all, our own. Powerfully written stories and narratives may begin a process of correction in our system of beliefs and categories by calling attention to neglected evidence and reminding readers of our common humanity. (p. 43)

I believe that our humanity is made visible when we reveal "games of truth" because this allows us recognise our acts of resistance to them and see why these acts matter. This was the case for Michael after one of our conversations. Writing in the transcript, he chose to reflect on something I had said in conversation: "The system worked exactly as it is designed, which is not for students like us."

> You know, this is something I have always been vocal about to varying degrees of success/ response, and I know logically and have experienced it, but you saying this was extremely validating. It's like, "Whew, okay, I knew I wasn't crazy".

Michael also highlighted a comment from me within the same conversation: "But you weren't even supposed to be found". Michael wrote:

> Powerful when you said it, and powerful now reading it back. These days, as I ponder and work through this stuff, I frequently come back to the idea of being a flower that bloomed in a dark room.

I wish I had thought to ask Michael about "being a flower that bloomed in a dark room" and what that meant to him. Why did he frequently come back to this idea? What sustained him in continuing to bloom even though he was in a dark room? How did he know he was finally blooming? He might have told me more about his acts of resistance to the demands of The Blob, which told him he wasn't meant to be highly intelligent because he was Black and that he was a threat because of it.

Challenging historical narratives

Historically, Black students have been considered less intelligent than students who are white, and the education system has been designed to ensure this narrative is reflected through its academic results and intelligence testing. Black people have learnt we must do more and do it better than everyone else in the hope of being seen as smart enough. Black children with neurodivergence don't fit neatly into this narrative. They are routinely punished for behaviours like excitement, passion, shyness or anxiety, which are interpreted by those in power as defiance, aggression, rudeness or unintelligence (Coral, 2024). These interpretations reinforce beliefs about Blackness and unintelligence, leading to lowered expectations for success, resulting in lower academic outcomes. These narratives won't change without interrogating our beliefs and intentionally changing our responses to them.

With my background as a gifted education teacher and lived experience as a highly intelligent Black student, I shared some of my knowledges to support Michael in deconstructing the discourses around Blackness and intelligence. When considering Michael's different intersecting identities, I asked questions about the "games of truth" that might be at play in his experience:

- Who is allowed to be intelligent in this society? Who isn't and why?
- What do we learn about intelligence from within the Black community?
- What narratives around Blackness and intelligence have changed over time?
- How have these changes benefited whiteness?
- How would the dominant culture benefit from you believing yourself to be a threat because of your intelligence?
- What kind of relationship do you want with your intelligence while being Black?

Understanding the power imbalances within society around Blackness and intelligence became pivotal for Michael in re-authoring a new narrative for himself. Moving the problem to a social context enabled him to see how Black boys were never considered to be smart, let alone smarter than any children who were white! He recognised how the Black community worked to resist the narrative of unintelligence by redefining and celebrating Black Excellence for their children, even when whiteness continued to demand perfection from them. This enabled him to reflect on what sustained him through his education journey on his quest to "escape from the demands of The Blob".

Michael: A lot of it was "We can't handle this, we can't answer your questions. We don't know how to support you, so we're just going to sequester you". And then for me, I've always been a fighter, so to speak, and I just never backed down from a conflict, so it was like, "Okay, now this person [meaning himself] is a threat". As opposed to thinking "Okay, this kid needs a little bit more multidisciplinary support, emotional support or different content" sort of things. It was more like "If he's not going to stay in line, we're going to keep him in line". And that's kind of when I realised that I couldn't escape, so I'm going to figure this puzzle out myself, and that helped me excel faster.

Sandra: So, you're starting to see things that are these patterns. Speaking up, knowing as much or more than your teachers, and they can't handle it. They don't know how to handle it. They don't know because they don't see you as being someone who should be as smart as that. You're not supposed to be as smart as that. People who are supposed to be as smart as that are white, are rich, you know? Not you. So that makes you defiant. But how else are you going to get their attention? You tried telling them, "I need more", but they didn't listen. They don't know because they don't see you as someone who should be as smart as that.

Michael and Sandra reflected on this dialogue in writing in the transcript.

Michael: Nailed it. Yup. Hard to stomach, but yeah.

Sandra: Yeah, I know, and it's completely the fault of the systems at play in society. The tests were never made to find you. Since you were noticed, that also meant you were wrong and something had to be blamed on you, too. (Yes, even as a kid, it had to be clear that somehow you were wrong because the system is based in whiteness, and it can't be wrong because it's "supreme/the best".)

Michael: Whew, so real again.

CRT recognises that the education system is working exactly as it's meant to. It creates more opportunities for white children to succeed by ensuring that fewer Black students do. Because of the systemic racism at play, Black people are held captive to narratives that may never change because they continue to benefit whiteness. The work of creating "pockets of freedom" involves learning and understanding the significance of historical narratives of race within the dominant culture. A culture of supremacy in which whiteness is considered the best creates an opposite that's positioned as the worst or the least. This "opposite" is Blackness (Coral, 2024). White supremacist narratives of Blackness don't change easily, and unless we actively challenge such beliefs and stories, they will negatively influence the healing environments we wish to create.

Intersectionality and anti-essentialism

To build a culture of co-creating stories with Michael, I needed to remember that even as people who were both Black and neurodivergent, there would still be significant differences and nuances in our experiences. Michael was from the US and grew up in a Black family within a wider Black community. I grew up as a transracial adoptee in Canada but resided in the UK. Although we had some parallel experiences, we had distinct differences in our relationships with the dominant culture. Reflecting on the overlapping privileges and oppressions I faced made me more

intentional about reducing the imbalance of power that often occurs within therapeutic spaces. Some questions guided my quest to become more decentred:

- What unconscious biases might I have about Michael's social identities that could affect my ability to see him as the expert on his experience?

- How can I avoid thinking that I have all the answers or that I am an expert on Michael's lived experience?

- How am I using my lived experience, skills and talents to support Michael in co-creating his preferred story?

- How am I growing my capacity to be willing to learn from Michael, trust in his skills and knowledges, make mistakes and be held accountable when I do?

- Who supports me when I must hold myself accountable, and in what ways do they help me?

Being intentional about how I engaged within the "pocket of freedom" supported my commitment to reducing the influence of dominant social discourses. I wanted to ensure Michael could safely explore alternative interpretations of his stories and clarify, further enrich, question and reflect on them through the transcripts of our conversation, rather than me interpreting his actions through my understanding of Blackness.

In one of our conversations, Michael said, "I just take care of people, kind of a big brother". In the transcript of this, we had the following written dialogue.

Michael: I actually like this about myself, that I can be people's big brother when they need it. I just feel like because I was protecting myself solo for so long, it eventually got taken advantage of, and in my desperate need for deep connection, I let it happen, whether consciously or unconsciously.

Sandra: This is where I have my biggest questions, but I'm not sure if this is what you'd want to explore more in the future. The gap between wanting to help and being so aware of the differences between you and others. Yet at the same time, struggling to find ways to fill that gap to find belonging (and at the expense of not listening/creating too many changes to yourself?). Not sure if that's what I want to say or not, but it's an initial thought for you to ponder or expand on to clarify for me if you want.

Michael: Yeah, for sure. These are the doors I need to open and recognise, and have been pondering over.

We're all influenced by the dominant culture in different ways. Our experiences shape how we interpret our actions and those of others, especially from more marginalised communities. Neutrality is not possible in therapeutic work. By doing nothing, we align ourselves with the narratives defined by the dominant culture. Questioning any biases or beliefs we might bring into the therapy rooms and asking for feedback throughout the conversation reminds us that we collaborate and are not experts on the lives of others. Black people are not a monolith, and our experiences of neurodivergence are not the same either. Yet, we are each uniquely qualified as experts on our own experiences.

Differential racialisation

Critical race theorists have drawn from different academic fields to create their framework, and they ask us to do the same when finding our path to liberation. There are many paths to freedom. Unlike whiteness, which doesn't believe it thinks and reasons from a white perspective, but from a universally valid one, which is "the truth" and everyone knows it (Baldwin, 1961), narrative therapy also draws on many different schools of thought. This gives us freedom to sculpt a therapeutic space that fits the person's needs, without relying on the tools and beliefs of the dominant culture to do so. This also helps ensure that progress isn't necessarily defined by whether it benefits whiteness.

Creating "pockets of freedom" entails finding "stories of resistance that are built on ... linked to and grounded in [Black] people's traditions, cultural practices and history" (Akinyela, 2025. p. 21). For Black people with neurodivergence, "progress" within therapeutic contexts and how it is achieved may be different from what we've been taught it *should be*. I had to intentionally refrain from assuming there was only one right answer to Michael's problems, and that I knew what it was. Michael needed to define what progress would look like for him. I wanted to be open-minded to the skills, values and commitments Michael appreciated in himself, even when the dominant culture might not have been so appreciative.

A component of Michael's dominant problem story was what he called his "Armour". This was a collection of protection and coping mechanisms created "to escape the demands of The Blob". This was mentioned frequently and was woven through many of our conversations.

Michael: It wasn't enough for people to just be like, "They're on something different". They don't have to hop on the cliff; that's fine, we can do it. There seems to be a mob that needs to keep saying, "Why don't you want to be like us?" "Why don't you want to do this?" They have to kind of like invalidate you to justify their role or experience. That's what I noticed, just in every social, family, friends, school, whatever, over time. And so, I guess it's exhausting trying to like ... You can only take so many arrows ... So you start to feel like, "I need to put something on when I leave that house. Because if I don't, you know, I'm going to bleed out. I'm dealing with too many arrows".

Sandra: What was the armour made of?

Michael: I think, charming, jokes and saying witty things was part of it. It was like, "Okay, yeah, that keeps them entertained. They won't bother me". And I think just a natural composure. When I was young, I was with my gang members and stuff, so I learnt how to stay composed, you know? I'm saying a roomful of people who may not respond to things the same way as other people ... You can't talk to a dude who caught a body [killed someone or had someone killed] the same way you would talk to somebody who's getting on your nerves in the store. And you've got to be very careful.

In the transcript of this conversation, Michael reflected:

This was a really dope question [What was the armour made of?]. It made me reframe and reflect in ways I haven't. I internalised a lot of negative stuff and turned my gifts into curses. Now it's hard to discern the difference.

Highlighting the double consciousness Michael experienced helped him acknowledge what he needed protection from while living within his different intersecting social identities. It allowed him to see his experiences differently, supporting the creation of a preferred story about himself and his intelligence.

Through my questions, Michael was "invited to be the one who [was] interpreting the experiences of [his] life" (Russell & Carey, 2004, p. 39). In this way, what Michael deemed important and preferred was centred, regardless of whether it aligned with dominant cultural ideology. From this point, Michael identified other situations in which he had intentionally used his intelligence to align with the values, hopes and principles he had for his life. This allowed him to begin building new identity conclusions.

Voices of colour

Storytelling plays a pivotal role within CRT, creating a way to "reduce alienation for members of excluded groups while offering opportunities for the dominant group to meet them halfway" (Delgado & Stefancic, 2001, p. 44). There can be a gap in understanding by therapists, counsellors and neurodiversity-affirming helpers who want to understand Black experiences of neurodivergence but have backgrounds, perspectives and experiences that are radically different. Through storytelling, we provide "a language to bridge the gaps in imagination and conception that give rise to the different" (Delgado & Stefancic, 2001, p. 44). Akinyela (2025) described the significance in African culture of "call and response", in which the storyteller and witnesses work together to tell and interpret a story. The story is only complete when there is a teller and a witness to it. For instance, in Black churches, someone leads the ceremony and is consistently joined by others to co-create the rhythm and meaning of what's being told.

Storytelling in narrative therapy enables the linking of lives around shared themes, values and beliefs, which supports the development of an alternative story that enables other possibilities for living. The practice of outsider witnessing introduces "a third party who is invited to listen to and acknowledge the preferred stories and identity claims of the person consulting the therapist" (Russell & Carey, 2004, p. 65). This practice further supported Michael in re-authoring the story of his intelligence. He asked Casey, his white nonbinary long-term partner, to act as an outsider witness to his preferred story.

Sandra: What parts of that story might be connected to part of your own story? Is there anything in that difference that maybe you could resonate with?

Casey: I resonate with being really intelligent. That's something that, as Michael has been working with you and doing self-worth, that I've noticed in myself, too. Like, "Oh, yeah, I kind of just discredit my intelligence as well". I don't notice all the time. I think I'm quick to second-guess my own voice.

Sandra: And did you find that Michael being able to own more of his intelligence and what it does for him, or has done for him, was something that you might give yourself more credit for in the future? Is that what you're saying?

Casey: Yeah, recognising like, "Wait! No, I can do this. Wait, no, I do have good ideas. Wait! I am smart. Why am I second-guessing myself?" But it's like, "Well, because those people are attacking you. And that's scary". So it's something I would like to hold my ground on, I guess, better. Kind of like, "No, I know what I'm standing for. And I know what I know. And you're not going to tell me I'm XYZ just because you don't agree or understand" … I need to acknowledge that sometimes people don't understand me because they're not there. And that's got nothing to do with me … And then just in confidence, Michael supports my confidence a lot. I was raised to like "not brag", but I think the flip side of that coin is that I never learnt how to cultivate my own pride and confidence in myself.

This conversation helped develop a double-storied narrative. Michael could look beyond the problems and difficulties he experienced to discover the special skills and knowledges that arose from responding to the hardships he had faced. He saw how his experience contributed to improvements for Casey's life, which further validated his new narrative of himself and his intelligence. Michael also saw how his experiences might be useful for other Black men dealing with similar situations to his.

Sandra: What were some things that stood out for you from what Casey shared about your story? What did they bring up for you?

Michael: They talked a lot about having the confidence to stand their ground, to be able to own certain things. And it's really, maybe, reassuring to hear. I'm glad I heard it. You know, through my journey, the thing that I needed and had a lot to help me do things was a certain confidence in certain things. Like, I've always known I was going to be good with words or something like that. I'm confident. … I value that a lot more now than I did before. I wonder if there's probably a lot of stressed-out young men out there who feel like, "Man, I don't want to have to be an asshole to be confident. I want to just be confident myself and know that I can come in there and like, 'I ain't gotta be showboaty to be valuable'". I didn't think I was providing the alternative to that as much as I was, so hearing it from Casey saying, "Oh, I can own that" makes me go, "Oh man, okay. That is something valuable to provide". It is good, you know?

Michael also connected what he learnt about himself from Casey to the wider Black community. He recalled some ancestral wisdom to enrich his preferred identity claims of his intelligence.

Michael: Nipsey [Hussle][5] said, "The highest human act is to inspire", so the fact that, okay, I can help somebody have the confidence to fight back when they should is like the goal I've always had, you know? It's in everything I do … Octavia Butler[6] made it okay to imagine something else. Not what's been given to you, but something completely, radically different. And that takes confidence and a lack of fear, and that's something that I always try to have at least that. So, to see that in [Casey's] eyes was cool. It's really, really important.

Linking lives through storytelling helped Michael develop stronger identity claims about his extremely high intelligence, while being a Black man. Having someone witness the new story of how he'd learnt to use his intelligence gave it more realness and authenticity. This happens when the telling of the story "is witnessed and responded to by a significant audience" (Russell & Carey, 2004, p. 67). Who Michael was and how he experienced neurodivergence created unique skills and insights to navigate hostile environments more safely and gave him the confidence to build an armour of coping strategies, ensuring his survival in many harmful and life-threatening situations. Michael saw how his hardships inspired others to find the confidence to "imagine something completely different against the demands of The Blob", and his experiences weren't for nothing. The skills and talents he acquired were valuable and important, and could continue to support him and others in the future.

Conclusion

There are many routes to liberation as we transform the relationship between race, neurodivergence and power. Each neurodivergent person has a unique path to take on this journey. But for Black people who navigate neurodivergence alongside the daily stresses of oppression, it becomes an exhausting, all-encompassing and often dangerous quest. When we need therapeutic spaces to rest and find solace, I hope that we'll find more "pockets of freedom" within them, spaces that empower us to reconnect to our communities, our culture, our ancestors and each other. Spaces where our unique knowledges, beliefs and skills are valued and our humanity is restored as we discover more preferred stories to sustain us. Spaces that enable us to return home to ourselves and, for a brief time, set us free.

Notes

[1] Some expressions of neurodivergence are more socially accepted than others. In this paper, I wanted to centre how being Black adds a unique layer of experience to living with any form of neurodivergence. Exploring different forms of neurodivergence and their relationships to race and power would take a whole series of books.

[2] Conversely, Black children in schools in which there is a low percentage of Black students have been over-diagnosed with "mental disorders" in comparison to their school's total population. They have also been diagnosed with "more severe" types of "mental disorder" (read: less "socially acceptable" and therefore further from access to power) compared to other (particularly white) students with the same presentations. Black children in schools with a higher proportion of Black students have tended to be underdiagnosed (see Coral, 2024).

[3] Identity and language play important roles in the neurodiversity movement. Many people, clinically or self-diagnosed, chose to use identity-first language (autistic person, ADHDer, dyslexic, etc.) to show that their neurodivergence isn't something they can or would choose to see as separate from themselves. However, for this paper, I have chosen to use person-first language in relation to the specific experiences of Black people navigating neurodivergence, unless referring to a person who identifies otherwise. Referring to "Black people with neurodivergence", rather than "neurodivergent Black people", is a way of highlighting these two realms of identity and their intersectionality to make visible Black people's specific experiences of neurodivergence. Race is seen first in the dominant culture. When race is not mentioned, whiteness is the default assumption. To say "men who are Black" would reify whiteness as the norm against which Blackness needs to be specified. In this paper, I use identity-first language for Blackness to centre the experience of Black people. I then consider how

neurodivergence and other social identity markers can compound our experiences of oppression.

4   I haven't heard of a similar use of transcripts in narrative therapy practice. With limited time with clients and my access needs, I have found reviewing transcripts of discussions to be a useful extension of therapeutic conversations as well as being helpful for my skill development and processing needs. I have noticed that many of the people I work with have also chosen to utilise the transcripts in various ways based on their access needs and preferences.

5   Nipsey Hussle was a Black American rapper and activist.

6   Octavia Butler was a Black American author of speculative fiction.

References

Adaway, D. (2019). *What exactly is critical race theory?* https://adawaygroup.com/critical-race-theory/

Akinyela, M. (2025). Decolonising our lives: Divining a postcolonial therapy. In M. Akinyela (Ed.), *Culture, politics, spirituality and practice: A book of resistance and critical theory for disturbing times* (pp. 5–30). Dulwich Centre Foundation.

Baldwin, J. (1961). *Nobody knows my name: More notes of a native son.* Dial Press.

Black Lives Matter. (n.d.). *About.* https://blacklivesmatter.com/about/

Bloom, H. (1998). Neurodiversity: On the neurological underpinnings of geekdom. *The Atlantic,* (September). https://www.theatlantic.com/magazine/archive/1998/09/neurodiversity/305909/

Coral, S. (2024). *It's never just ADHD: Finding the child behind the label.* Sage.

Crenshaw, K. (1989). Demarginalizing the intersection of race and sex: A Black feminist critique of antidiscrimination doctrine, feminist theory and antiracist politics. *University of Chicago Legal Forum,* (1), 139–167.

Delgado, R., & Stefancic, J. (2001). *Critical race theory: An introduction.* New York University Press.

Fanon, F. (1967). *Black skin, white masks.* Grove.

Foucault, M. (1997). The ethics of the concern for self as practice of freedom. In P. Rabinow (Ed.), *Michel Foucault: Ethics: Subjectivity and truth* (Vol. 1, pp. 281–302). New Press.

Hammoud-Beckett, S. (2007). Azima ila Hayati – An invitation into my life: Narrative conversations about sexual identity. *International Journal of Narrative Therapy and Community Work,* (1), 29–39.

Jones, K., & Okun, T. (2001). *Dismantling Racism: A Workbook for Social Change Groups.* Change Work.

Menakem, R. (2017). *My grandmother's hands: Racialized trauma and the pathway to mending our hearts and bodies.* Penguin.

Okun, T. (2021). *White supremacy culture.* Dismantling Racism Works. https://www.dismantlingracism.org/white-supremacy-culture.html

Reddy, A. (2008). The eugenic origins of IQ testing: Implications for post-Atkins litigation. *DePaul Law Review, 57*(3), 667–677.

Russell, S., & Carey, M. (2004). *Narrative therapy: Responding to your questions.* Dulwich Centre Publications.

Singer, J. (1998). *Odd people in: The birth of community amongst people on the autistic spectrum: A personal expiration of a new social movement based on neurological diversity* [Unpublished honours thesis]. University of Technology, Sydney.

Singer, J. (2024, December 20). Revealed: Who "really" coined "neurodiversity"? An evidence based corrective. *Reflections on Neurodiversity.* https://neurodiversity2.blogspot.com/2024/12/revealed-who-really-coined.html

Taylor, B. (2019, November 24). Intersectionality 101: What is it and why is it important? *Womankind Worldwide.* https://www.womankind.org.uk/intersectionality-101-what-is-it-and-why-is-it-important/

Walker, N. (2021). *Neuroqueer heresies: Notes on the neurodiversity paradigm, autistic empowerment, and postnormal possibilities.* Autonomous Press.

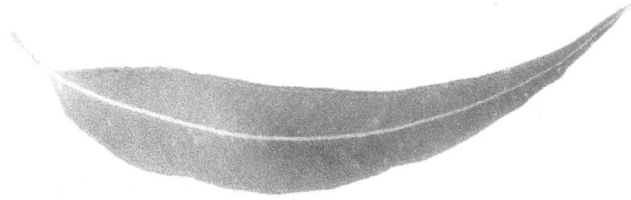

Children's problems and children's solutions:
Celebrating the agency of neurodivergent children

by Tarang Kaur

Tarang Kaur is a developmental therapist with Children First India. She works with children across a range of neurodevelopmental and socioemotional challenges using child-led and play-based approaches. Tarang graduated from Lady Shri Ram College, New Delhi, and completed her postgraduate studies at the University of Delhi. tarang.cf@gmail.com

ORCID ID: https://orcid.org/0009-0008-0463-7224

Abstract

Children, particularly those on the neurodivergence spectrum, have historically not been afforded a great degree of power and voice in their own lives. This has significant implications for the therapeutic space, in which the identification of "problems" and interventions to address them may not take the child's perspective and skills into account. My work seeks to explore children's views and understandings of their "problems", as well as the uniquely skilful actions they take in response. In this paper I describe how narrative therapy principles were adapted for children across a wide spectrum of social skills and degrees of access to spoken language to document – in the form of a scrapbook – various experience-near descriptions of children's problems and children's solutions. This living document records the skills, values and acts of resistance demonstrated by a community of neurodivergent children, and offers an opportunity to witness this community's agency and unique insight into their own situations.

Key words: neurodivergence; autism; nonspeaking; nonverbal; children; collective document; therapeutic document; narrative therapy; narrative practice

Kaur, T. (2025). Children's problems and children's solutions. *International Journal of Narrative Therapy and Community Work*, (2), 73–85. https://doi.org/10.4320/VQGM2915

Author pronouns: she/her

Cultural narratives around children tend to do them a disservice by treating them as naïve or immature beings without much experience of the world. Meanwhile, the "grown-ups" around them are assumed to know what's best. Coupled with very little freedom and agency in terms of legal rights, these dominant discourses marginalise young people and frequently strip them of their power and voice (White, 2000).

This becomes doubly true for children who are neurodivergent – notably, those on the autism spectrum. Certain societal discourses that further the control and marginalisation of children's lives can be observed. For instance, certain modes of communication are considered more socially desirable and "valid" than others: the acquisition of verbal language is a highly sought-after goal in "autism-as-deficit" models (Tager-Flusberg & Kasari, 2013). Nonverbal or assisted communication, in comparison, may be seen as second-tier: we may not prioritise "hearing" what a child is trying to communicate when that communication is happening without spoken language. For instance, when a child is pointing to a door, crying and resisting any attempts to bring them into a room, we may still try to bring the child into the room. It is only when the child says "I don't want to go in this room" that they might (might!) be afforded the dignity of being heard.

Others may also decide for a child what passes for an "action" – executed with intention, with depth and meaning, and serving some purpose – as distinct from what can be dismissed as a "behaviour" – a surface manifestation that must be analysed for "assessment" or "management" (White, 2000). Such discourses withhold consideration of the meanings of children's actions and may instead note only "behaviours" and "symptoms" that don't signify the child's comprehension or values. This furthers an understanding of autism as a deficit, resulting in a plan of intervention or "treatment" that disregards the skills and knowledges generated by neurodivergent children through their own lived experiences of the world (White, 2000).

As a person active in the field of early intervention, I find that it is especially important to be cognizant of these prevailing discourses, and to be careful to not further biases and unequal power relationships under the guise of treatment and therapy. Instead of situating "autism" as the problem in and of itself, a more "experience-near" intervention might consider what children understand to be their difficulties, and explore actions and solutions that have been protective for them, through their own lived experiences of coping and management (Olinger, 2021b).

Documenting children's perspectives and knowledges

Within the context of developmental therapies with neurodivergent children – especially those less fluent with spoken language – there may be an inclination to identify so-called "symptoms" as the "problems" to be addressed. These "symptoms" may include "emotional regulation", "inappropriate behaviours", "meltdowns", and so on. However, this view demonstrates little curiosity for eliciting experience-near accounts of what young people *actually* view to be their "problems", and how their actions reflect skills of coping.

My practice has been to apply the principles of narrative therapy to view children as engaging not in meaningless or problematic "behaviours", but in meaningful, intentional "actions" that serve some protective purpose. To this end, I created a scrapbook to use as a collective living document recording children's descriptions of their struggles, accompanied by the strategies and solutions that they have developed.

Reflecting the ways in which these experiences were elicited and recorded as per the different profiles and needs of the children, the scrapbook is divided into the following sections:

- Section 1: Descriptions of children's problems and children's solutions, as explored through externalising conversations, predominantly with children who were comfortable talking about their problems

- Section 2: Descriptions of problems and subsequent acts of resistance with children who found spoken expression to be challenging or limiting

- Section 3: Descriptions of problems and subsequent acts of resistance with children who didn't speak or spoke very little.

This paper explores the creation of each section of this collective document, including the methods and adaptations that were essential to eliciting the children's voices as collaborators and uplifting their lived experiences and insider knowledges.

Scrapbook Section 1:
Documenting the knowledges of
children who were comfortable
speaking about their problems

This section includes accounts from children who found it beneficial to engage with externalising conversations to describe their problems, and who spoke about the strategies they employed to overcome them.

Describing children's problems

Externalising conversations, alongside supplementary modalities like art and drama, were used to personify the problem and locate it outside the child and their identity (Carey & Russell, 2002). Rather than imposing experience-distant labels ("emotional dysregulation", "meltdowns", "aggressive behaviour" and so on), I sought to explore and record the child's own experience of the problem: "The Angry Feeling", "Chest Hurty" and so on.

The statement of position (SOP) maps – in particular, *SOP map version 1* (Morgan, 2006) – offered a framework, as follows.

Characterising the problem

When identifying and naming a "problem" as an external entity, building characters around feelings offered a relatable starting point for many children. The simple question of "What name can we give to the feeling that comes when this happens?" was often the most helpful one, as it created a comfortable distance between the child's experience and the feeling that they perceived as unclear or undesirable.

Questions about the situations in which the problem arose also aided its description and characterisation:

- When does [problem name] come?
  What makes it come visit?

- When is it the strongest?

- When is it weaker?

- When does it go away?

In addition to such questions and conversations, the process of characterising a problem was supported by other modalities such as:

- *art and images* – drawing a body figure and asking the child where a particular feeling or problem

lived; drawing feelings as characters that visit in various situations; using flashcards

- *embodiment and drama* – acting out how it feels in the body and face when a certain feeling comes to visit, where it is felt in the body; for instance, based on a child's description of how "meltdowns" felt, we were able to name the problem "Chest Hurty"

- *picking up on the child's language and scaffolding responses* – for instance, noticing a child using the word "rubbish" when she felt frustrated or embarrassed allowed us to talk about and build a character around the "Rubbish Feeling"

- *turning adjectives into nouns* – Even the simple act of adding a "the" to the start of a feeling, and calling it an "it", created comfort in children.

Many of the young people I worked with adopted a defensive, protective posture when asked if they got angry. But by beginning to call it "The Angry Feeling" instead of "getting angry", and other similar externalisations, a lot of children were immediately more relaxed about talking about this character.

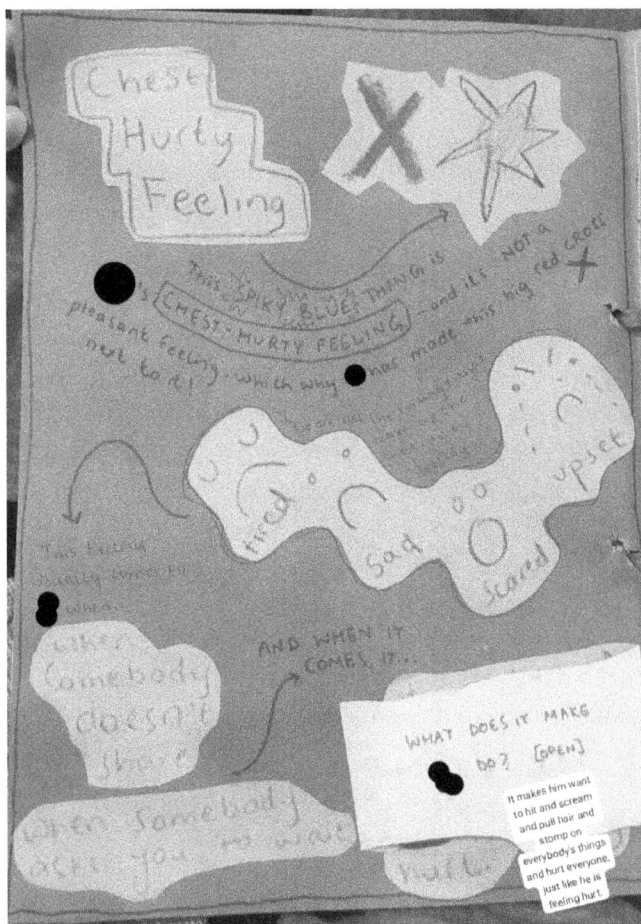

Figure 1. Characterising The Chest Hurty Feeling to describe Aarav's[1] experience of "meltdowns", as documented collaboratively in the scrapbook.

It seemed to signal to them that they were not being blamed, and that there was genuine curiosity about this experience – which seemed to be a radical act for many.

Such explorations proved helpful in the identification and naming of problems in experience-near ways that centred the children's perspectives on their struggles.

Mapping the effects of the problem

To build a richer understanding of the problem, it also proved important to identify and elaborate on its effects:

- What happens when [problem name] visits?

- What does it want you to do?

Figure 2. Adi's depiction of what happens when "Fighting" comes to visit: "It makes me hit and shout at a friend! Now the friend is sad. And angry at me."

Evaluating the consequences

With the effects of the problem better fleshed out, children can be invited to take a position on these effects: whether they are okay with what the problem is doing or not. This invitation was oftentimes revelatory for children, as they realised that they could take a stance on something that was previously considered an inextricable part of their identity!

Some questions that invited children to evaluate the consequences of the problem were:

- Does it feel okay when [problem name] comes or not?

- Do you like having [problem name] around?

- Do you like what [problem name] is doing?

- When [problem name] is doing this, is it being nice or not nice?

- What happens when it comes
  … when you're at school?
  … when you're at home/with Mumma or Papa?
  … when you're with friends?
  … and so on.

Drawing the child's attention to a previous situation when the problem may have come up helped them to recall the associated effects. This was particularly helpful for children facing difficulties in abstract thinking and the "mental time-travel" required to think back to an experience and emotional state in the past (Barresi & Moore, 1996).

As children shared their experiences, writing or drawing descriptions made it easier for them to remember, refer to and stay with these ideas over time.

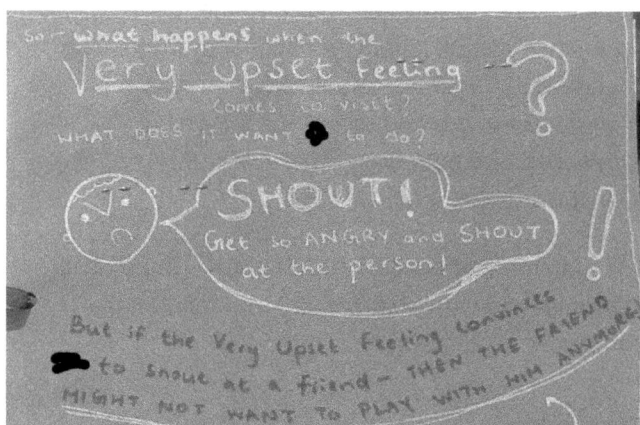

Figure 3. I noted down Jai's words as he described what happens when the "Very Upset Feeling" comes to visit, and we later documented this in the scrapbook.

While asking such questions, it was also important to let the children know that they had the option of answering "sometimes", "something else", or even "I don't know". Giving children a pen and inviting them to physically interact with the effects previously noted down or drawn – for instance, putting a "tick" on what's okay and a "cross" on what's not, or drawing emoji-style faces to indicate a feeling – also made it easier for them to indicate their position in relation to the problem and its effects.

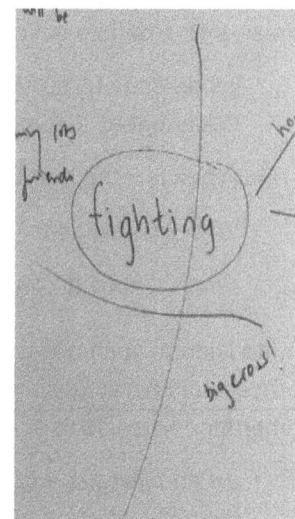

Figure 4. "Fighting is badmaash [naughty]!" Adi shouts while drawing a cross on the word. "Big cross!"

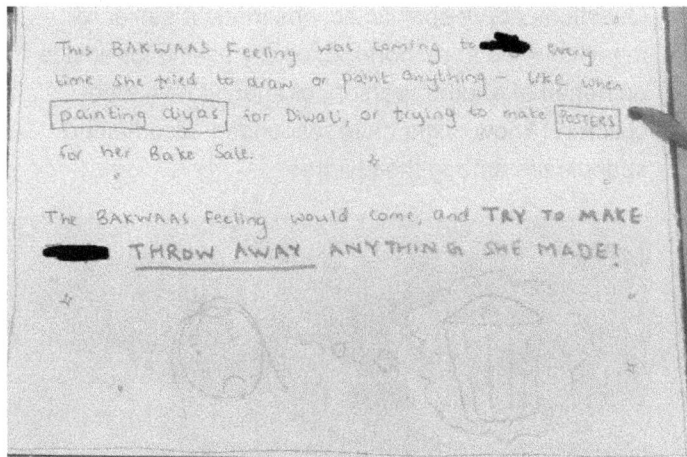

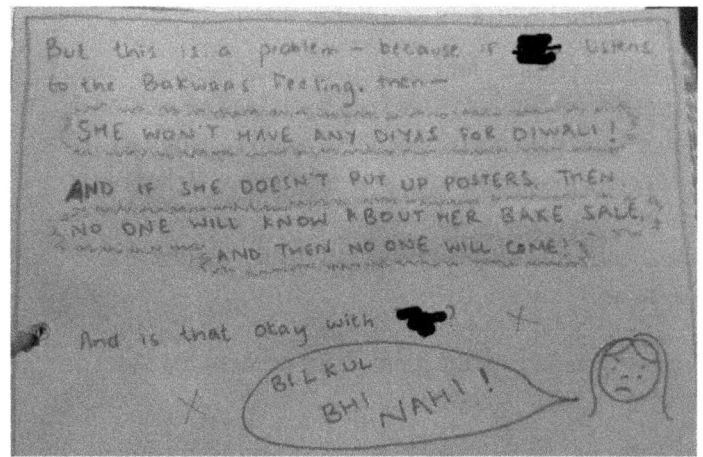

Figure 5. Riya and I talked about The "Bakwaas [Rubbish] Feeling" that was making her dislike and throw away all the posters she made for her bake sale. But if she didn't make and display posters, how would people come? When considered this way, Riya – who previously wanted to stop making the posters altogether – decided that this was totally unacceptable. She was not at all okay with this effect of The Bakwaas Feeling!

A nonjudgemental and curious attitude proved crucial when facilitating such evaluations. People may have certain expectations about what constitutes a "correct" evaluation; for instance, if The Angry Feeling makes a child shout and hit when it visits, then they "ought" to not be okay with what it is doing. However, a child's indication that they are okay with having this character around can once again be examined as an action, rather than a behaviour. The so-called problem may serve some useful or protective function. What if The Angry Feeling keeps the child feeling safe in scary situations? Or perhaps it helps them get the things they want! Without maintaining a posture of curiosity and openness, the subtleties of detangling the beneficial effects of a situation from the harmful may be lost.

Justifying the evaluation

Evaluating the effects of the problem offers a natural entryway into a justification of the evaluation. The question "Are you okay with this?" is easily followed by "Why?", and subsequently, "What values does this position reflect?"

Oftentimes, evaluations had already been offered implicitly or indirectly by the child. In these cases, making explicit what is implicit was helpful. This could be done using a smorgasbord approach, where options were listed based on what the child had already shared, and the child was invited to choose the best fit.

For instance, according to Adi, Fighting is "badmaash" (naughty) because it makes him do hitting and shouting, which makes his friends sad and angry. I observed, "It seems that you don't want to fight with your friends – what can we call that?" At this point, we get a chance to

discuss ideas like "getting along", "being friendly" and "making friends happy" as options. "So not fighting with friends is important for you – and it seems like getting along is important to you!" I surmised. Adi agreed, and shared that he wanted to make his friends happy because "I love my friends!"

Summarising what we had learnt about the child in the third person, or through the voice of another person or character, and then asking the child to comment as an outsider, was also often helpful in prompting a justification of these evaluations.

Tarang: What would you call a boy who's five years old and wants to be with his friends very badly, and have fun with them and make them happy?

Adi: Friendly and nice. He is a good boy.

Tarang: I see. Well, didn't you say you also want to have fun with your friends, and make them happy too? Does that make you a friendly and nice boy, too?

Adi: Yes, I want to be friendly. I will take care of my friends and be nice to them. My mom and dad say you have to be friends forever, like Optimus Prime and Bumblebee![2]

A process of *re-authoring* thus began as we elicited Adi's values, the history of these values, and the actions he had taken in line with these values to overcome the problem or lessen its effects (Carey & Russell, 2002).

Describing children's solutions

By asking children for solutions to problems they have experienced, we could reiterate their position and values and help build a second story of resistance. Collecting these solutions and suggestions honoured children as experts in their own lives, with unique skills and knowledges arising out of their values and histories.

These questions made it easier for children to reflect on their actions:

- When did [problem name] go away or get smaller?

- What powers did you use to make it smaller?

These questions explicitly drew children's attention to their own acts of resistance and regulation, and positioned them as active agents standing up to problems or their unwanted effects. Framing their actions as the use of "superpowers", "special abilities", "brainpower" or other such metaphors, usually helped – most of them were very excited to talk about their actions in this manner!

- Then what did you do when [situation] happened?

Questions about specific actions made it easier for many children to respond. Explicitly asking for advice on behalf of another person, or sharing how other children I know might have responded, also helped spark ideas among the children.

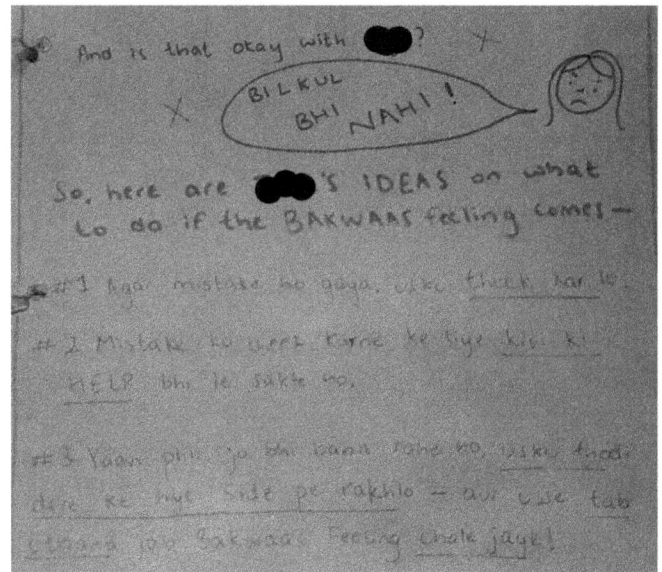

Figure 6. Some of Riya's suggestions about what to do when The Bakwaas [Rubbish] Feeling comes. #1 If you make a mistake, fix it; #2 Take someone's help to fix the mistake; #3 Keep it to the side for a while and pick it up when The Bakwaas Feeling goes away!

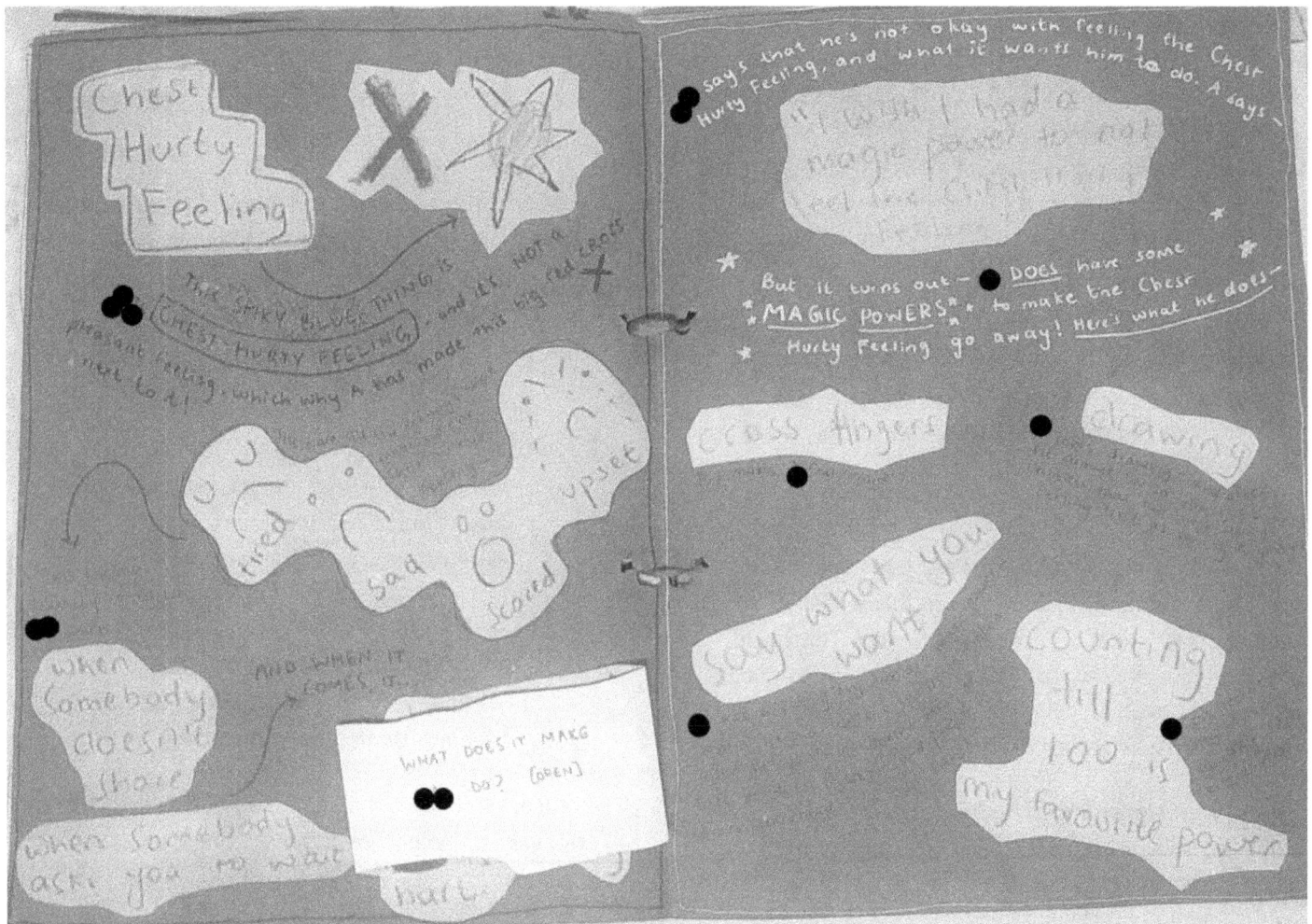

Figure 7. Aarav's "magic powers" that can make The Chest Hurty Feeling go away.

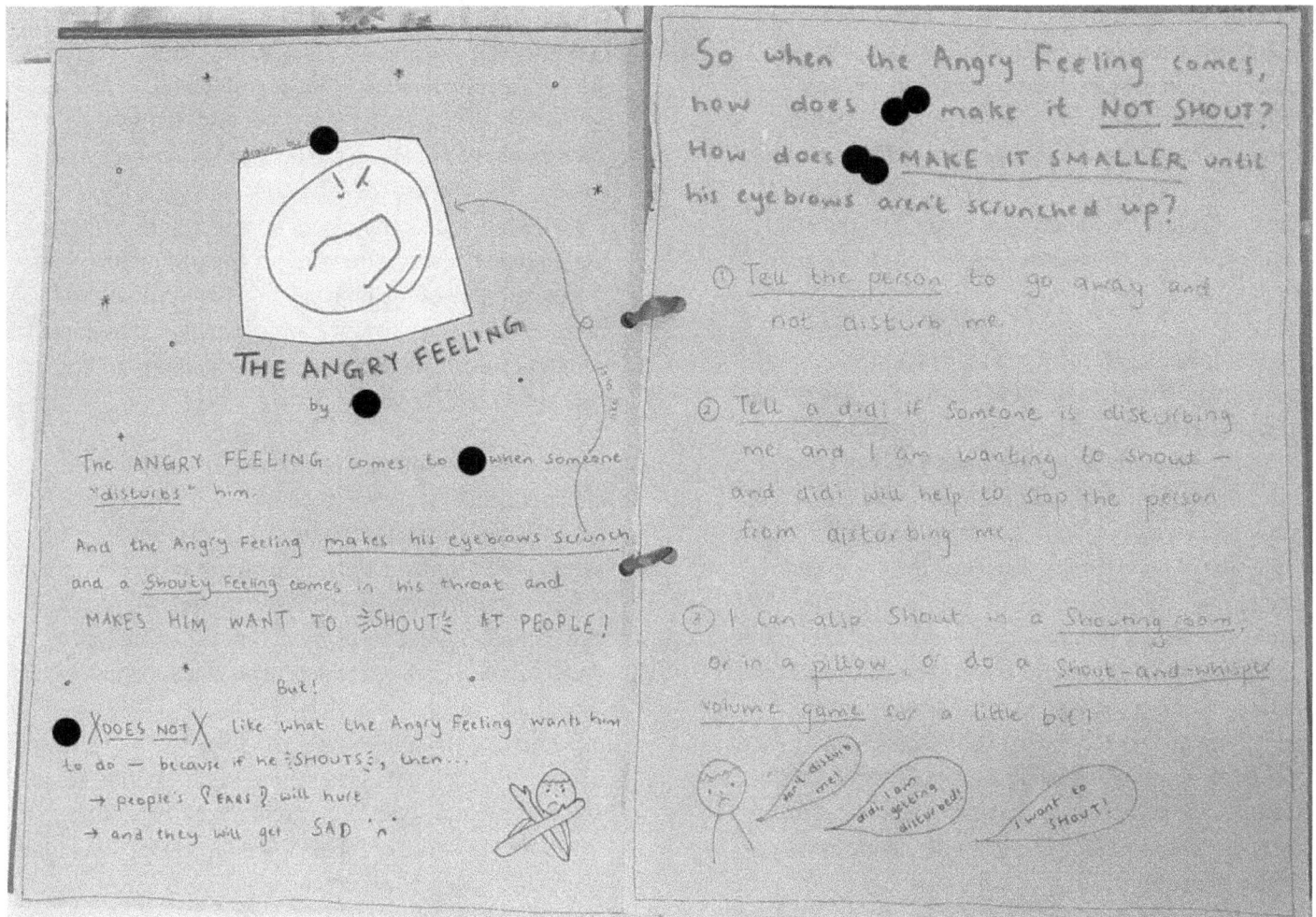

Figure 8. Prabir's suggestions about how to deal with The Angry Feeling that comes when someone disturbs him.

When collating strategies for overcoming the problem, it helped to tell my young collaborators about the existence and intent of the scrapbook, which fostered a sense of togetherness and community. Many children were quite empathetic, and eager and proud to give suggestions if they felt that some other child needed their assistance for a problem that *they* were uniquely equipped to deal with!

Scrapbook Section 2: Documenting the knowledges of children who were less comfortable with speaking

This section of the scrapbook includes descriptions from children who may demonstrate foundational skills of social communication, but for whom spoken expression and communication may feel limiting or challenging. Here I describe how principles of narrative therapy offered alternative perspectives on their difficulties and subsequent acts of resistance.

Of the various cultural narratives that marginalise neurodivergent children, a significant one is the *abilities* discourse in which others decide what expectations to hold of a person who "looks normal" or appears "capable", regardless of how much support they *actually* need (Olinger, 2021a). Such expectations are especially problematic for children who demonstrate some rudimentary skills of social communication and spoken language, to the extent that they may be viewed as "normal" or "relatively able" by those around them, which ultimately dictates the level of support and consideration they are (or aren't) offered. For instance, consider Ayush, a young autistic boy experiencing high anxiety and difficulties with emotional regulation, who nonetheless had a brief repertoire of spoken language, often present as templated or scripted speech. When he would collapse to the ground, crying and struggling to make sense of why he was upset and how to calm down, he tended to scream a few phrases over and over again (e.g., "I want Mumma! I want Mumma!"). At this point, rather than considering a neurodivergent child's needs, others tended to be taken aback and critical of what they perceived to be a "tantrum". Since he was often taken at first glance to be a neurotypical kid, they tended to expect "better" from him.

A traditional deficit-based model of intervention may look at this situation and identify the skills that are "lacking", which would then be targeted for "correction" through an intervention. In such a model, however, both the *problem* and the *skills required to overcome it* are identified by outsiders – without much interest in the skills and knowledges generated by the child, based on their own unique experiences of the world (White, 2000).

An alternative to this approach may be to instead try to spot what the *child* views as a difficulty, and remain as experience-near as possible in this description to facilitate understanding of the child's acts of resistance to the difficulty. In Ayush's case, we talked about "emotional dysregulation" as a shorthand description of the gist of his difficulty. However, this term wasn't able to capture his experience. For instance, he might be saying "I want Mumma!", but even when his mother would come, he'd continue crying (sometimes even harder!). Looking only at "emotional dysregulation" didn't help us figure out what could actually *help* – that clue came from Ayush himself when we noticed him doing something peculiar. Sometimes, when starting to cry, he'd lightly slap himself on his hand and start saying, "I got hurt!"

This could have been seen as a symptom or "behaviour" – that he's getting dysregulated and crying; he's hurting himself, or at least pretending to; we need to get him to stop doing this "I got hurt" behaviour. This would have closed the door on exploring Ayush's experience. Instead, describing this as an *action* invited us to look at Ayush as an agent in his own life, acting to serve some need of his own. What might be *his* experience of the difficulty that we were calling "emotional dysregulation"? What was *he* experiencing as a "problem", and how might this "getting hurt" action be helping him respond?

We started considering: could it be that, when Ayush is experiencing what we're calling "dysregulation", his struggle is that he's not able to make sense of his situation? Perhaps a slap on the hand was helping him localise an otherwise generalised, undefined feeling into something that could be addressed. With this understanding, the next time he hit himself and told us, "I got hurt", instead of telling him "Nothing happened" or "Don't do it next time", we got out a First Aid box and affirmed: "Ayush got hurt – where does it hurt?" We put some "medicine" (sanitiser) on his "hurt" and applied a "band-aid" (a scrap of tape). We noticed that this ritual helped him calm down immensely.

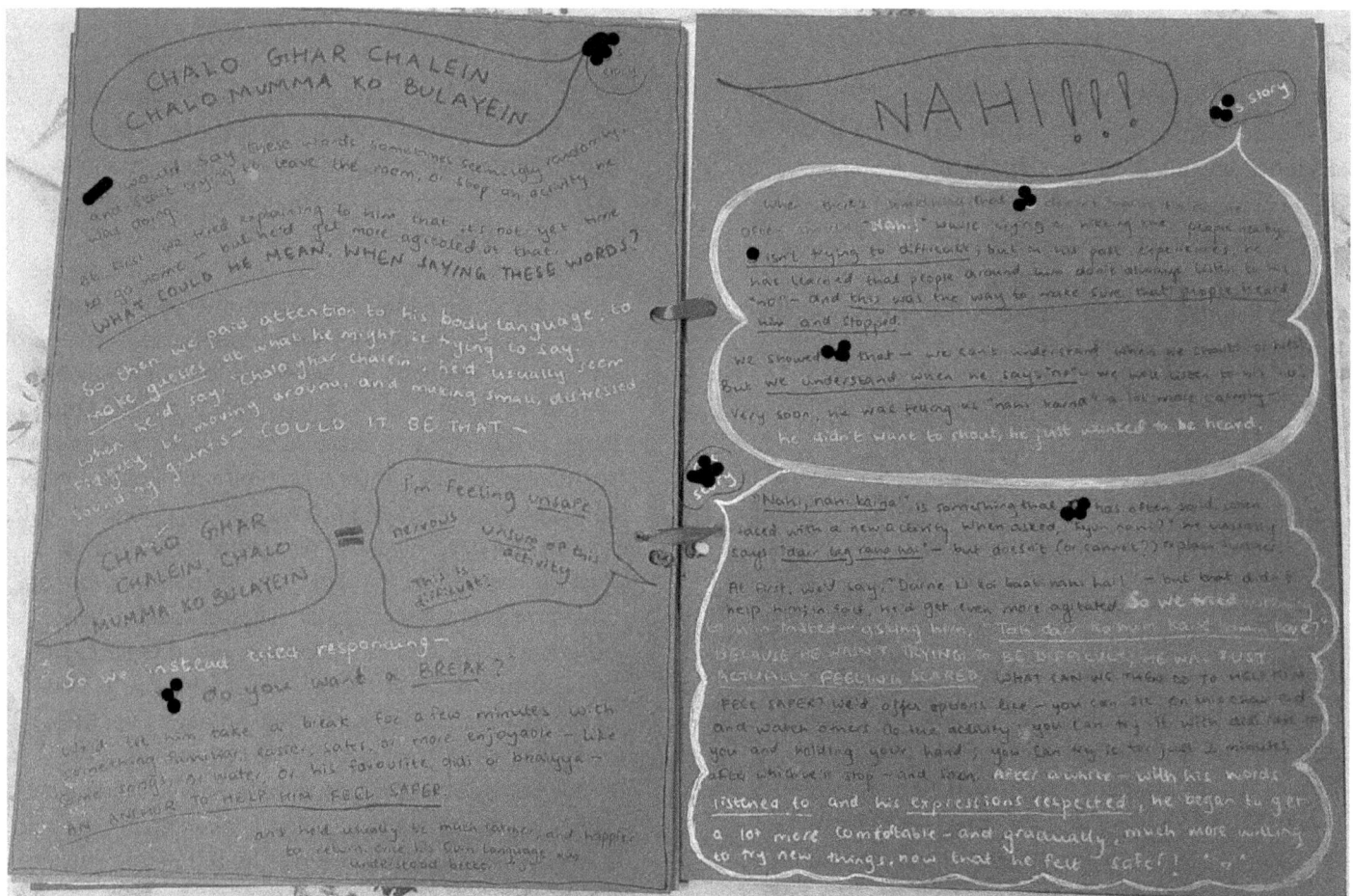

Figure 9. A page from Section 2 of the scrapbook describing stories similar to Ayush's.

Over time, when Ayush became "dysregulated" – for instance, crying for his mother even when she was there with him – we began to ask him, "Where does it hurt?" He could understand and connect to this phrase, take action to make himself feel better by getting his First Aid box, and express his feelings in a way that made sense to *him*: "I got hurt".

This approach recognised the child as having unique skills and capacities – and showed curiosity about the child's understanding of the problem. This helped mitigate against the creation of a pathologised single-story. In fact, what we may otherwise have identified as a "problematic behaviour" could be recognised as an act of strength and resistance!

Stories of neurodivergent children using their own language and words to describe their experience of a struggle were documented in Section 2 of the scrapbook, with the hope of offering an alternative lens for viewing children's problems and recognising acts that could serve as self-initiated "solutions".

Scrapbook Section 3: Documenting the knowledges of children who don't use speech

This section of the scrapbook includes descriptions of children who are nonspeaking or minimally speaking, with limited foundational skills of social communication. Principles of narrative therapy offered ways to identify and highlight their acts of resistance.

Words – "explanations" – are often used as the critical differentiator between an action and a behaviour. Unfortunately, this means that those who don't use words can't explain or justify a "behaviour" in a way that would be seen as elevating it to the status of "action". They may be subsequently stripped of their status as intentional agents (Olinger, 2021a; White, 2000). This can make young neurodivergent children particularly vulnerable – especially those who are nonspeaking and those who may have limited avenues for social communication through alternatives like augmentative and assistive communication (AAC). This group of young people is most easily dismissed

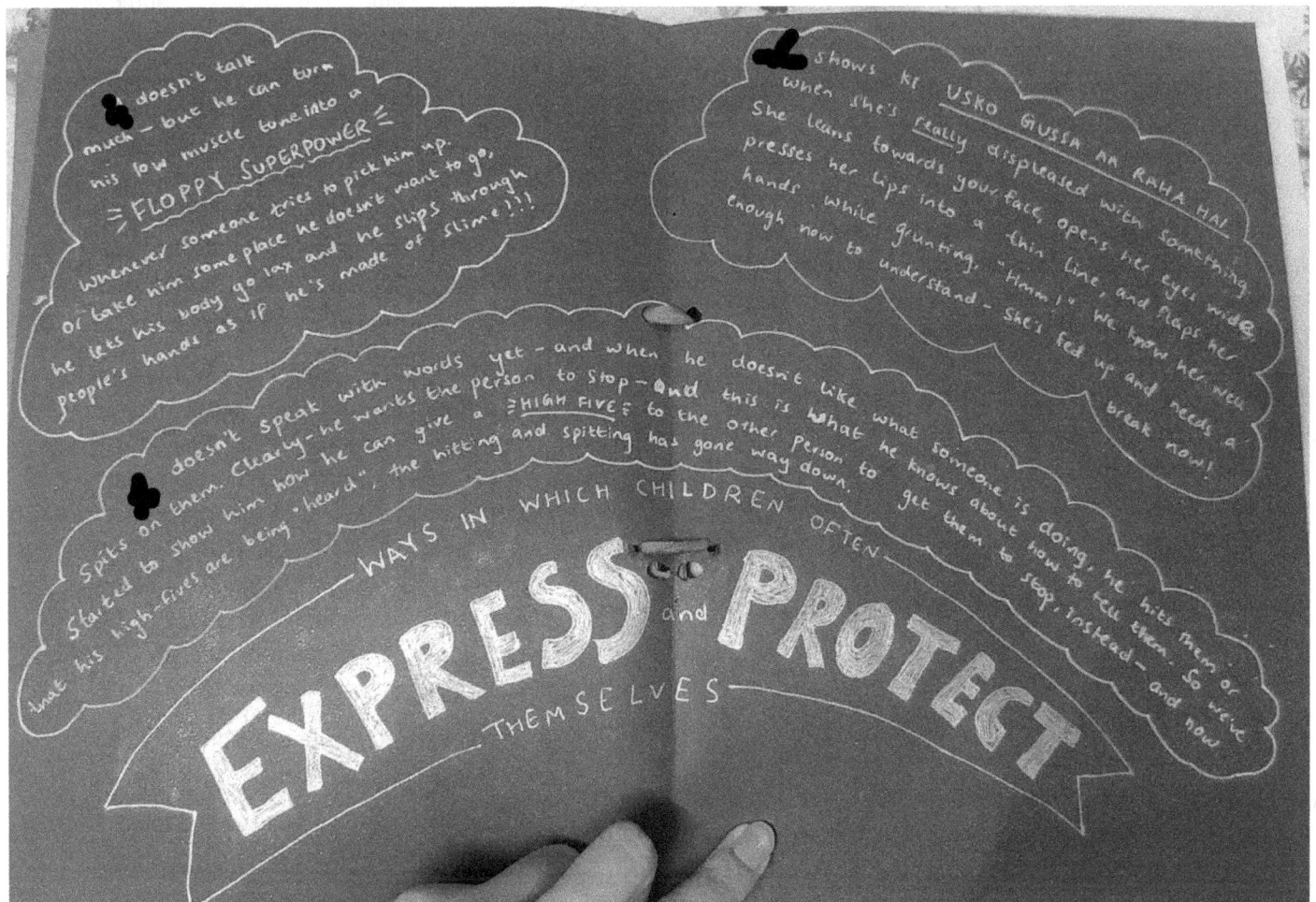

Figure 10. A page from Section 3 of the scrapbook documenting a "Floppy superpower" and other ways of communicating.

when formal language is privileged. When working with such populations with the intention of "intervention", it's essential to be aware of these discourses – and we must thus redirect attention to the numerous actions that neurodivergent children take to protect and express themselves.

Henri was a four-year-old boy who didn't use words to talk. When people tried to pick him up to take him some place he didn't want to go, he would let his entire body go lax and slip through their hands as if he were made of slime! He might not *say* "no" through spoken language, but his *body* language was loud and clear to anyone willing to listen.

Similarly, Saurabh babbled but was otherwise nonspeaking. When he was feeling agitated, his face furrowed, he chattered emphatically, and he made eye contact with the offending person as he kicked or pinched them. These were obviously not desirable outcomes for the person across from Saurabh – but at the same time, viewing this merely as a "behaviour" would not capture the whole picture, either. There was intentional communication and "action" in what he was doing – a communication that went beyond the use of words.

We can maintain a focus on what such are actions might be "saying" and respond accordingly. "I'm not liking this, Saurabh", we may say as we block or redirect a hit. "If you want me to stop, you can give a high-five and we'll take a break." Though he still pinches or kicks at times, over time, as his high-fives were "heard", he began to pause and became quick to respond when offered a high-five, relaxing when the person responded by taking a step back.

Section 3 of the scrapbook documents several such instances to offer examples of ways we can reconsider our perspective when working with people who don't use speech, and how we can consider their "behaviours" as experience-informed *actions*.

Turns out – children are always, *always,* responding!

Reflections on power

My developmental work with children differs from more traditional counselling approaches in one key aspect: many of my young clients don't come in with an explicit self-identified problem. They may not even understand what we are supposed to be working on during our play

classes. This means that *I* am often the one identifying the so-called "problems" to be brought into awareness and discussion. This would put any therapist in a precarious position of power, where they could far too easily be incorrect in speaking for a child who might not be able to correct them.

To safeguard against this, I practise various systems of "checks" with children who can express themselves through language. Aside from verbal confirmations to ensure that the child and I are on the same page, examples of checks include explicitly telling children to interrupt me if they don't agree with or like what I said, including offering for them to give me a "thumbs up" or "thumbs down" if what I'm suggesting sounds good or not. This may take any other form that is familiar and relevant to the child – for instance, one child who loved computer games and programs said "cancel!" and "delete!" if he didn't like what I said! I also seek to include plenty of scaffolding through a smorgasbord of options or specific action-oriented questions to make my queries more understandable to younger kids. Bringing in multiple mediums – art, enactment, stories, and so on – also helps to reduce demand on abstract and verbal processing.

Difficulties around emotional processing and regulation are a common theme with the children I work with. "Feeling characters" (anger, embarrassment, disappointment, frustration, and so on) come up regularly. I quickly discovered that talking about "the feeling" and creating a character around it was often more relatable to the children, rather than building fictionalised personifications like I had initially hoped to elicit: "Dementor", "Black Hole", "Pocket Monster" (Quek, 2017), and so on.

I initially worried that approaching a feeling-based character as the "problem" would result in the *emotion* itself being viewed negatively – so I took care to ensure that we didn't take an adversarial position against it, rarely referring to the feeling as "the problem" directly, and instead focusing on the outcomes or situations that co-occurred with it. Rich descriptions arose from discussions of such feeling characters. When we explored a child's feelings with curiosity and a nonjudgemental manner, children often:

- found it easier to notice and articulate the experience of the emotion

- more easily understand cause-and-effect linkages between the feeling and its consequences

- demonstrated less resistance towards the emotion in question.

Often, the feeling characters were a crucial starting point in reaching a more specific understanding of a problem. For instance, Prabir and I initially started with "The Angry Feeling", which most notably would make him shout at others. After a while, this character morphed into the "Throat Vibration", referring to the feeling in his throat that came when he wanted to shout. Here, The Angry Feeling had to be understood before we could identify where the more specific "problem" – that is, shouting or the Throat Vibration – came from.

Navigating power and privilege, and taking care not to speak "over" a child, has been even more fraught when extending my work to children who are nonspeaking or minimally speaking, and those who may find fluent spoken communication to be challenging.

Some augmentative tools that expand communication beyond verbal exchanges – such as using "thumbs up" or "thumbs down", using flashcards, drawing pictures, engaging in enactments or nonverbal gestures – have been helpful for both speaking and nonspeaking children. Aside from this, however, none of the children and families I work with have used high-tech AAC devices or systems. Thus, I am in a precarious position of translating into words what someone is communicating to me *without* words.

At my place of work, we often try to differentiate a "spot" – an undeniable observation, like Ayush crying "I want Mumma!" or Henri's body going lax when you try to pick him up – from an "inference" about what that might mean. A desire to be decentred informs this differentiation, as we do not want to give our interpretations a position of primacy. However, some degree of interpretation is inevitable. There is no "pure" version of an individual's experience that can be accessed; some degree of mediation always exists when we try to understand what we observe. When working with children, especially those who are neurodivergent and nonspeaking, such mediation exists to a much higher degree. This is a dilemma I have had to grapple with.

When working with children with whom traditional systems of "checks" are harder to apply, I seek to stay as experience-near as possible by focusing on "spots" wherever I can. Inevitably, however, some interpretation and guesswork are needed by stakeholders in a child's life. If a child is crying or appearing to be in distress, it isn't enough to "spot" this; we have to hazard a guess as to what they may want or need. Do they need food, or rest, or quiet, or something else? Some measure of

translation will be needed if we cannot communicate with each other using the same language. However, I hope I have made clear the tentative nature of these interpretations: they are not absolutes but hypotheses aimed at serving the child's needs.

My intention in the stories documented in Sections 2 and 3 of the scrapbook has not been to speak "for" those who may not as easily speak for themselves; it is to provide an alternative lens through which to understand and interpret children's *actions*; witnessing them not as naïve or uncooperative beings, but as agents acting according to their own understandings and difficulties. This is an awareness that anyone working with children in a position of power – especially interventionists such as myself – need to hold.

In our personal conversations as a team of early-years developmental therapists, we often wonder whether the children we work with will return years later and tell us what they were thinking, feeling and experiencing back when we worked with them. It's very possible that we might not have got it "right". But I hope it'll be worth something that at least people were recognising that meaningfulness *was* there, and were at least *trying* to understand.

Archiving and sharing children's knowledges

Documents can ensure that words and ephemeral conversations "don't fade and disappear" (Fox, 2003, p. 27). Especially with children, having a record that they can refer to during situations of difficulty has proved invaluable in making their insider knowledges accessible to themselves: reminding them of how well they know their own struggles and what they can do in challenging circumstances. The scrapbook we have developed also offers a "children's community": a place where children can explore the advice given by other children and offer advice in turn.

Inviting children (and others!) to view this co-created scrapbook also applies a lens of appreciative inquiry (McAdam & Lang, 2003). The scrapbook testifies to the ways in which children use their agency during situations of difficulty. Through such ability-spotting, there is the uncovering and affirmation of the pride, capability and preferred identities of children. This is an opportunity for children to witness themselves as wielders of knowledge (Quek, 2017) and for others to witness them as capable and meaningful actors.

Honouring the idea of identity as a social project, we acknowledge how family and caregivers serve as a primary context where children's stories of identity are told, retold and co-created (Freedman, 2014). By involving the immediate family as witnesses to the child's experience, we invite them into the co-construction of preferred identities (Carey & Russell, 2003; McAdam & Lang, 2003; Morgan, 2006).

Outsider witnessing practices can be applied to facilitate this presence of third parties who acknowledge and thus help thicken preferred identities (Carey & Russell, 2003). Readers of the scrapbook are invited to witness the stories it holds through an included "prompt-card", which was formulated based on Michael White's map for outsider-witness responses (Carey & Russell, 2003; Denborough, 2008; Morgan, 2006; White, 2002).

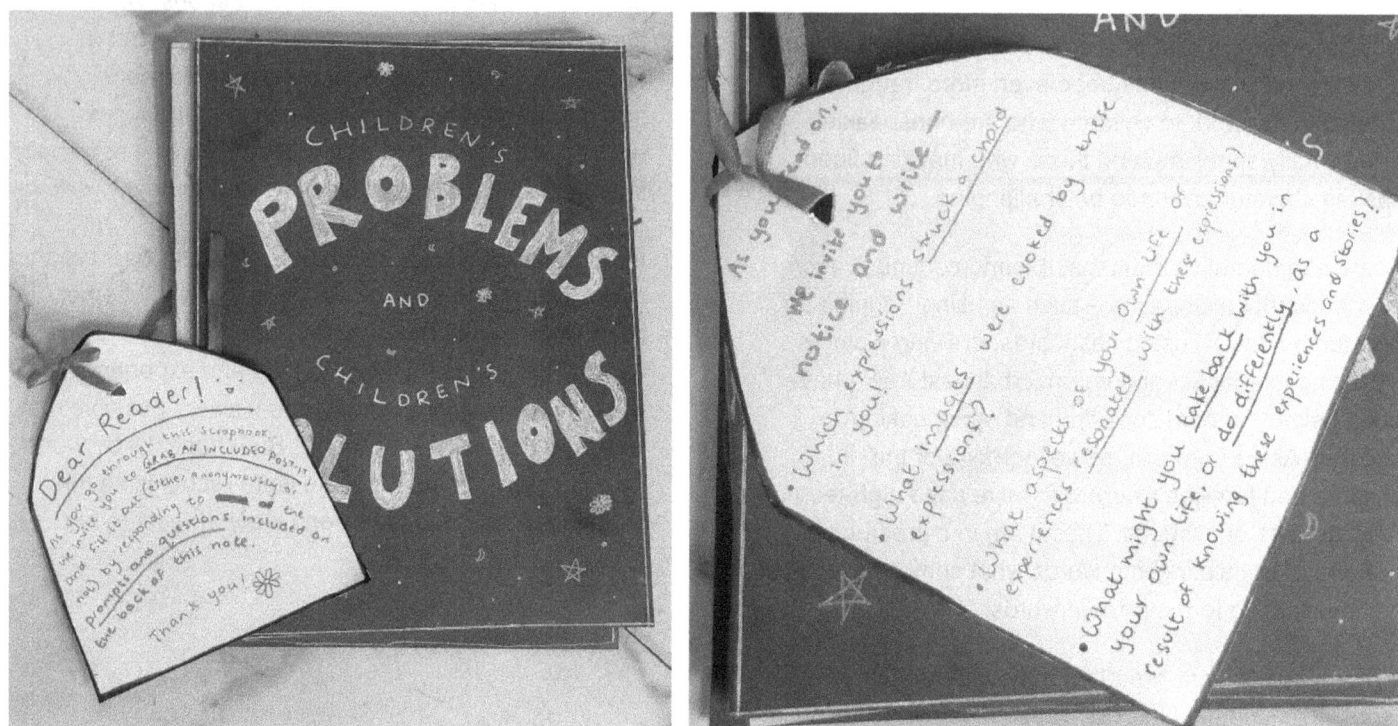

Figure 11. The scrapbook with its attached invitation for readers to witness and respond to the stories it holds.

Readers are asked to notice and write on sticky notes:

- Which expressions struck a chord in you? *(Identifying the expression)*

- What images were evoked by these expressions? *(Describing the image)*

- What aspects of your own life or experiences resonated with these expressions? *(Embodying responses)*

- What might you take back to your own life, or do differently, as a result of knowing these expressions and stories? *(Acknowledging transport)*

Children can go through the scrapbook later and read these witnessing accounts via the sticky notes. This enables them to witness their witnessing audience, thus furthering the idea of identity being a social co-construction. They can also witness their own impact and influence on a larger community with which they have shared their experiences and knowledge.

By creating this scrapbook as a collective document to record experience-near descriptions of children's problems and children's solutions, aside from its practical benefit as a repository of knowledge, it is hoped that we can help foster a sense of shared community among young people; make it possible to re-author problem-saturated narratives; and develop second-stories of the expertise and strengths in actions of a group that has, historically, not been seen as the experts in their own lives!

Acknowledgments

First and foremost, I would like to acknowledge all the young people with whom I have worked, who have so generously let me glimpse their stories and lives, and their valuable insights and knowledges. I would also like to extend my sincerest gratitude to Dr Shelja Sen and Ms Maya Sen for their mentorship and support in this project, as well as Dulwich Centre and Children First India for facilitating my learning in the field of narrative therapy. Last but never least, for their constant and steadfast support, I have many thanks to give to my parents, friends and partner.

Notes

[1] Names have been changed to protect the privacy of children and clients.

[2] These are characters from the "Transformers" media and toy franchise (e.g. Orci et al., 2010–2013).

References

Barresi, J., & Moore, C. (1996). Intentional relations and social understanding. *Behavioral and Brain Sciences*, *19*(1), 107–122. https://doi.org/10.1017/s0140525x00041790

Carey, M., & Russell, S. (2002). Externalising: Commonly asked questions. *International Journal of Narrative Therapy and Community Work*, (2), 76–84.

Carey, M., & Russell, S. (2003). Outsider-witness practices: Some answers to commonly asked questions. *International Journal of Narrative Therapy and Community Work*, (1), 3–16.

Denborough, D. (2008). *Collective narrative practice*. Dulwich Centre Publications.

Fox, H. (2003). Using therapeutic documents: A review. *International Journal of Narrative Therapy and Community Work*, (4), 25–35.

Freedman, J. (2014). Witnessing and positioning: Structuring narrative therapy with families and couples. *Australian and New Zealand Journal of Family Therapy*, *35*(1), 20–30. https://doi.org/10.1002/anzf.1043

McAdam, E., & Lang, P. (2003). Working in the worlds of children: Growing, schools, families, communities through imagining. *International Journal of Narrative Therapy and Community Work*, (4), 48–57.

Morgan, A. (2006). Creating audiences for children's preferred stories. In M. White & A. Morgan (Eds.), *Narrative therapy with children and their families* (pp. 99–119). Dulwich Centre Publications.

Orci, R., Kurtzman, A., Kline, J., & Davis, S. (Executive Producers). (2010–2013). *Transformers: Prime* [TV series]. Polygon Pictures; Hasbro.

Olinger, C. (2021a). Narrative practices and autism: Part 1: Theory and engagement: Shedding ableism from therapy. *International Journal of Narrative Therapy and Community Work*, (2), 32–41.

Olinger, C. (2021b). Narrative practices and autism: Part 2: Expanding on understandings of autism. *International Journal of Narrative Therapy and Community Work*, (2), 42–49.

Quek, E. S. M. (2017). Presenting the League of Parents and Small People Against Pocket Kering: Debuting the skills and knowledges of those who experience financial difficulties. *International Journal of Narrative Therapy and Community Work*, (3), 85–99.

Tager-Flusberg, H., & Kasari, C. (2013). Minimally verbal school-aged children with autism spectrum disorder: The neglected end of the spectrum. *Autism research*, *6*(6), 468–478. https://doi.org/10.1002/aur.1329

White, M. (2000). Children, children's culture, and therapy. In M. White (Ed.), *Reflections on narrative practice: Essays and interviews* (pp. 3–24). Dulwich Centre Publications.

White, M. (2002). *Workshop notes*. https://www.dulwichcentre.com.au/michael-white-workshop-notes.pdf

White, M. (2006). Narrative practice with families with children: Externalising conversations revisited. In M. White & A. Morgan (Eds.), *Narrative therapy with children and their families* (pp. 1–56). Dulwich Centre Publications

Review Essays

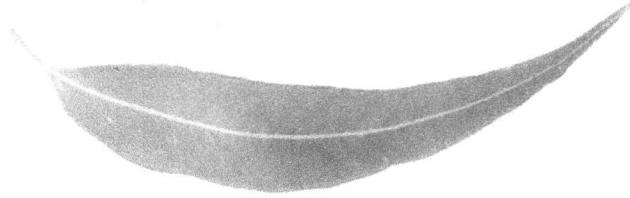

Opening our minds:

An alternative way of responding to personal and collective despair

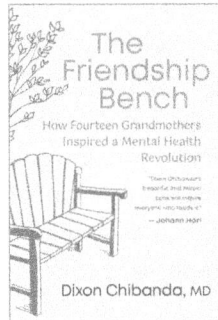

A review of *The Friendship Bench:
How fourteen grandmothers inspired
a mental health revolution*
by Dixon Chibanda

The
Friendship
Bench

How Fourteen Grandmothers
Inspired a Mental Health
Revolution

Dixon Chibanda, MD

Reviewed by David Denborough

David Denborough (dd) works at Dulwich Centre as a narrative practitioner with individuals, groups and communities who have experienced hardships, and also coordinates the Master of Narrative Therapy and Community Work program at The University of Melbourne.
daviddenborough@dulwichcentre.com.au

ORCID ID: https://orcid.org/0000-0002-3041-3135

Abstract

David Denborough reviews Dixon Chibanda's (2025) book, *The Friendship Bench: How fourteen grandmothers inspired a mental health revolution*. New World Library. 240 pp. ISBN 978-1-95583-102-4 (print); 978-1-95583-103-1 (ebook); 978-1-95583-117-8 (audio).

Key words: Friendship Bench; Dixon Chibanda; Zimbabwe; Africa; decolonizing; local knowledge; peer; book; review; narrative therapy; narrative practice

Denborough, D. (2025). Opening our minds: An alternative way of responding to personal and collective despair, a review of The Friendship Bench: How fourteen grandmothers inspired a mental health revolution by Dixon Chibanda. *International Journal of Narrative Therapy and Community Work*, (2), 87–90. https://doi.org/10.4320/IWFY2523

Author pronouns: All pronouns welcome

Picture this. It's a dry, warm winter's day in Zimbabwe. We are driving across dirt roads under big blue skies to the relatively new urban settlement of Hopley.[1] The poverty is striking. Only after I return to Australia do I learn that Hopley was established by the Government of Zimbabwe 20 years ago following Operation Murambatsvina[2], which is a Shona phrase meaning "remove filth".

The effects of Operation Murambatsvina are described by local psychiatrist Dixon Chibanda like this:

> The siege lasted just a few months, but the damage was done: by the time Murambatsvina was over, seven hundred thousand people were homeless, and an estimated two million had been psychologically impacted … We had been plunged collectively into a national crisis, and the only way out was through. (Chibanda, 2025, p. 30)

Twenty years ago, Dixon Chibanda found his way through in collaboration with 14 grandmothers and initially one Friendship Bench where those in despair could meet with a volunteer grandmother as an alternative to mainstream mental health responses. There are now Friendship Benches in communities across Zimbabwe (and beyond).

When we arrived in Hopley, we were greeted in song by two grandmothers, one grandfather and three local residents whose lives have been quietly, but significantly, transformed through their meetings on Friendship Benches.

One local resident described how she was suicidal before the grandmother sitting next to her "closed the grave I had dug for myself". This is a phrase I think I will always remember.

As we sat together in Hopley, I had a copy of Dixon Chibanda's new book in my satchel: *The Friendship Bench: How fourteen grandmothers inspired a mental health revolution.* When our meeting drew to a close, I asked if our hosts would each sign this newly published book and they kindly obliged. Later that day, when Cheryl White and I met with Dixon Chibanda at the new Friendship Bench Hub[3] in Harare, he added his signature. Looking now at these seven signatures, they seem a fitting symbol of significant collaborations between a psychiatrist and a local community. It's the accounts of these collaborations that are most moving to me in this book. In particular, how Dixon Chibanda has carefully and honourably acknowledged the contributions of the initial 14 grandmothers in the development of what is a unique approach.

Sometimes, a thin version of the Friendship Bench story is told, in which it's said that the grandmothers were *taught* Western cognitive behavioural therapy (CBT) and that this is what they then *deliver* on the Friendship Benches. But this book tells a much richer and more interesting story.

It describes how Dixon Chibanda, in collaboration with a collective of local Indigenous knowledge holders (grandmothers), collaboratively developed and articulated a local response to social suffering. It was Grandmother Jack who declared "Our people have always used the outdoors to share stories and resolve conflict" (p. 46) which led to the idea of outdoor benches. And it was the grandmothers who decided that the benches would not be called "Mental Health Benches" but instead "Friendship Benches". It was Grandmother Hwiza who emphasised the significance of song and dance in their approach, and Grandmother Chinhoyi who refused to work with material that was not written in the local Shona language: "Emotional problems are best said in your own language" (p. 51).

The collective of local Indigenous knowledge holders (grandmothers) did not always agree with each other, but through spirited discussions they created "a philosophy of care" (p. 113) and in careful and respectful collaboration with Dixon Chibanda developed their own concepts to describe their approach to healing. Within this tender-hearted book, it's possible to read about their three-part healing process, which Grandmother Jack describes:

> The three most relevant steps that help us to address these issues are *kuvhura pfungwa* [opening the mind], *kusimudzira* [to uplift], and *kusimbisa* [to strengthen]. These are the three most important pillars of the therapy we provide on the bench! (p. 67)

Initially, this process involves a volunteer grandmother meeting a person at one of the Friendship Benches and receiving and responding to their stories of suffering. The grandmothers (and now some grandfathers) "immerse themselves" in people's stories (isn't that a beautiful concept!) and as Grandmother Kusi describes, they use the person's own language "to give them hope" (p. 108). This includes listening to and honouring the stories brought to the grandmothers, including the local idioms used to convey and share suffering such as "I have a painful heart" or "my spirit has abandoned me"

(p. 70) or *kufungisisa* (meaning over-thinking). And as Grandmother Kusi describes, this process involves "making people feel respected and understood, regardless of their money or status of the problems they bring to the bench" (p. 54).

Significantly, the process also involves joining people together in peer support/action groups called Circle Kubatana Tose (meaning "holding hands together" in Shona), which then spark and sustain income-generating projects.

It's an approach that involves personal, emotional, social *and* economic empowerment, and it's one that has now sparked the imagination of many people. These days, the Friendship Bench team receive many visitors. Knowing this, we thought we'd better come prepared with a song to offer in return. If you have ever been to Zimbabwe, you might be familiar with Zimbabweans' exquisite harmonic singing skills. It's a somewhat intimidating place to sing! Luckily, the folks in Hopley were gracious and kind and perhaps a little surprised that the Australians had brought a song.

To the grandmothers of The Friendship Bench

We've come from across the seas
To the Friendship Bench and CKT
[Circle Kubatana Tose]
We've heard the legend of Gogo Jack
So we've travelled a long way down this track

Kuvhura pfungwa
Kusimudzira
Kusimbisa

You're opening our minds
You're opening our minds

Zimbabwe is a special place and one that has known, and still knows, great suffering. All the grandmothers involved in the creation of the Friendship Bench approach had tended to family members dying of HIV/AIDS. Around the same time as Operation Murambatsvina, the Tree of Life narrative approach[4] was developed in response to children in Matabeleland whose families had been devastated by HIV/AIDS (see Denborough, 2008; Ncube, 2006). Dixon Chibanda's book is tender and poignant as he writes his own experiences of heartbreak and friendship into the story. He evocatively describes how the Friendship Bench approach was "bootstrapped from scarce resources and a broken heart" (p. 134).

Dixon Chibanda has wider dreams now, of contributing to de-medicalising responses to mental health in other countries and contexts (the Friendship Bench approach is now being engaged with in a number of countries). He is also looking to generate forms of research, through the African Mental Health Research Initiative, that can explore people's experiences of wellbeing in local African cultural terms. This is including efforts to create a "Hope index". If such an index already existed, it would have been able to measure a marked increase in my sense of hope after our visit!

It seems appropriate to return to the words of the grandmothers and grandfather whom we met in Hopley. When we asked them if they would like to send a message to grandmothers in Australia who might be thinking of establishing a similar Friendship Bench project, here were their responses:

One grandmother said, "This job requires you to be a confidential person, to know that the stories shared on the bench are not to be shared with anyone else. You also have to be someone who is empathic, and to be someone who is very good at listening. To do the job well requires more listening, less talking. Sometimes you will come across tough stories, and this requires you to be a strong person. But you shouldn't be a person who is judgemental or who advises people what to do. We do not offer advice but assist people to come up with their own solutions. This is a beautiful job. It's very enjoyable. And we need sometimes to be humble."

A second grandmother said, "We wish we could have some exchange visits with grandmothers in Australia and other places! We could learn from each other and then learn to use all the different methods that grandmothers from different cultures are creating."

And the grandfather said, "To the male counsellors, it's important to know that most men do not open up. They are shy to open up. But men are also suffering, and too often they are suffering alone. They do not talk about it. As men, please be open to share problems so that we can find solutions together."

Many communities in different parts of the world are struggling with problems related to mental health, and the medicalising of suffering seems to be making things much worse rather than better. The grandmothers of the Friendship Bench and Dixon Chibanda have a different approach to share. Theirs is a story of honouring and articulating healing ways from Indigenous knowledge holders. It's also a story of turning to community members rather than professionals to receive personal stories of suffering and then link these stories to collectives of peer support and economic action. Theirs is also a story of people in their elder years, not retiring, but instead continuing to offer so much to the younger generations.

I am left with this poignant image:

> Often, I'd see a grandmother slowly trudging, with measured steps and absolute determination to her bench – usually with the help of a grandchild, who would return a few hours later to walk her home. (p. 172)

A number of the initial grandmothers have passed on now, but through this beautiful book by Dixon Chibanda, their knowledge and stories and contributions will be forever known.

Acknowledgments

Cheryl White and David Denborough would like to acknowledge the team from the Friendship Bench who took us to Hopley for their kindness and thoughtful conversations: Jesca Tapfumaneyi, Mutsa Mazarura, Portia Chiuyu and Chadzamira Muchemwa.

Notes

[1] Hopley is also known as Hopley Farm Settlement. To read more about its history and living conditions, see Abraham R. Matamanda (2020).

[2] To read more about Operation Murambatsvina and its effects, see Potts (2006).

[3] To learn more about the Friendship Bench Hub and organisation, please see their website: https://www.friendshipbench.org/

[4] To learn more about the Tree of Life Narrative Approach, see: www.dulwichcentre.com.au/tree-of-life

References

Chibanda, D. (2025). *The Friendship Bench: How fourteen grandmothers inspired a mental health revolution.* New World Library.

Denborough, D. (2008). *Collective narrative practice: Responding to individuals, groups and communities who have experienced trauma.* Dulwich Centre Publications.

Matamanda, A. R. (2020). Living in an emerging settlement: the story of Hopley Farm Settlement, Harare Zimbabwe. *Urban Forum, 31,* 473–487. https://doi.org/10.1007/s12132-020-09394-5

Ncube, N. (2006). The Tree of Life Project: Using narrative ideas in work with vulnerable children in Southern Africa. *International Journal of Narrative Therapy and Community Work,* (1), 3–16.

Potts, D. (2006). "Restoring order"? Operation Murambatsvina and the urban crisis in Zimbabwe. *Journal of Southern African Studies, 32*(2), 273–291.

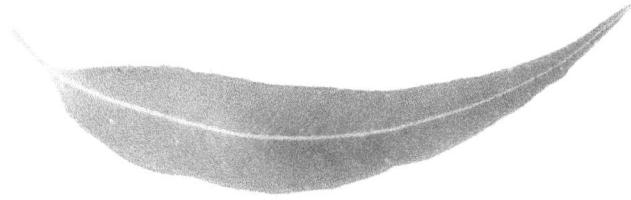

We all become witnesses:

An alternative way of responding to personal and collective despair

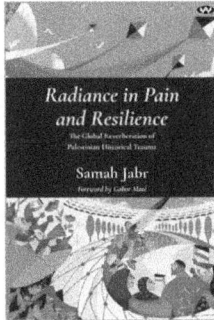

A review of *Radiance in Pain and Resilience:*
The global reverberation of
Palestinian historical trauma
by Samah Jabr

Reviewed by David Denborough

David Denborough (dd) works at Dulwich Centre as a narrative practitioner with individuals, groups and communities who have experienced hardships, and also coordinates the Master of Narrative Therapy and Community Work program at The University of Melbourne. daviddenborough@dulwichcentre.com.au

ORCID ID: https://orcid.org/0000-0002-3041-3135

Abstract

David Denborough reviews Samah Jabr's (2025) book *Radiance in pain and resilience: The global reverberation of Palestinian historical trauma*. Wakefield Press. 304pp. ISBN 9781923042926.

Key words: Palestine; book; review; narrative therapy; narrative practice

Denborough, D. (2025). We all become witnesses: A review of Radiance in Pain and Resilience: The global reverberation of Palestinian historical trauma by Samah Jabr. *International Journal of Narrative Therapy and Community Work*, (2), 91–94. https://doi.org/10.4320/EXRT5001

Author pronouns: All pronouns welcome

"In a world gone mad, we need books."

So says editor Julia Beaven as she introduces Dr Samah Jabr at the global launch of her new book, *Radiance in pain and resilience: The global reverberation of Palestinian historical trauma*. I sense that everyone in this room at the University of South Australia can relate to Julia's words.

This book has been published by Wakefield Press, a small independent publisher based here in Tarntanya Adelaide. By some measures, we are a world away from Jerusalem, where Dr Samah usually lives and works. But one of the main messages of this book is about the reverberation of Palestinian stories, the significance of bearing witness to them and, significantly, what this can make possible. As Dr Samah described during the launch, "We can generate very important lessons from Palestine".

There were many moving moments tonight. One being when Dr Samah explained why she has written the pieces that have been compiled into this collection. She spoke of how her work as a Palestinian psychiatrist means that she is witness to unrelenting stories of injustice. Witnessing, she says, has a significant meaning both in liberation psychology and within Islam. Bearing witness can be an act of responsibility, of justice-seeking and of healing. It is both secular obligation and sacred duty. Writing about her work, sharing Palestinian testimonies of daily injustices, means that Dr Samah's readers become witnesses by proxy:

> Writing helps me to organise my feelings and my thoughts about all that I receive from people. I also feel a professional ethical responsibility which matches with my Islamic ethical responsibility. When I share testimonies, this is a way for me to share these responsibilities – to pass this to others. It enables others to become witnesses.

And so it is that all of us in this room, and all who read this book, become witnesses, and the stories of Palestine reverberate and spark new meanings and actions.

Crucially, Dr Samah invites us to be witnesses in particular ways:

> Palestinians need the solidarity of others who recognize us as active subjects and fighters for freedom, not as bleeding victims. (Jabr, 2025, p. 99)

Related to this, during the launch, Jon Jureidini asked Dr Samah to convey to us the significance of the concept of *Sumud,* which is the term Palestinians use to express their steadfastness and resistance:

> Palestinians have used the term *Sumud* since the time of their defiance of the British mandate, and it expresses both a state of mind and an orientation to action. Everyone in Palestine understands *Sumud*, but finds it difficult to convey to others. Usually Palestinians hold a symbol of *Sumud* as an old olive tree that is deeply rooted in the land. It is not an inborn trait or the consequence of a single life event, but a system of skills and habits that are learnt and can be developed. It forms the basis of a lifestyle of endurance. We have a responsibility to try to research *Sumud*[1] and to support it.

I am particularly interested in Dr Samah's vision for forms of collective therapeutic practice that support *Sumud*:

> Practitioners can focus on *Sumud* (steadfastness), solidarity, redress, resistance, accountability, narratives, storytelling, and community healing, contributing to addressing collective trauma beyond clinical definitions. Such efforts aim to rebuild social fabric, validate experiences, and promote resilience. (Jabr, 2025, p. 71)

As *Sumud* involves "collective action, strong community ties, solidarity" (Jabr, 2025, p. 239), Dr Samah convincingly argues that work to alleviate mental health struggles requires collective approaches:

> In the end, addressing collective trauma requires comprehensive approaches that go beyond clinical models. They need to embrace cultural, historical and communal healing practices – while acknowledging the systemic injustices of perpetuating suffering. We have to empower the Palestinian community to address mental health as a form of resistance against the occupation on our minds. (Jabr, 2025, p. 71)

As an example of a collective response, Dr Samah and her colleagues Zaynab Hinnawi and Elizabeth Berger have recently published a paper called "Healing through the skies" (Jabr, Hinnawi, & Berger, 2024), which describes a therapeutic group activity for Palestinian children based on creating and flying kites. As I read this paper, I kept thinking of colleagues from the Remedial Education Center and School of

Salaam Children of the Olive Tree in Jabalia in the north of Gaza, which no longer exist due to devastating bombing by the IDF since 7 October 2023. Back in 2012 and 2015 when a team from Dulwich Centre Foundation visited this team, we learnt a lot from them about the significance of kites in Gaza. When we shared with them the Kite of Life[2] they came up with their own creative version:

> We have three new inventions for the Kite of Life that we also want to share with you! We decided that the frills or ribbons on the sides of the kite can represent "the things in life that lift us up". The frame of the kite can represent "what

keeps our life in balance". And here in Gaza, we sometimes place small messages on the string of the kite. The wind then carries these messages up the string, as if they are climbing into the air. We decided that we will include on our kites a message to the next generation. We hope you like these Palestinian inventions!

> … We are writing to you from Gaza, Palestine. We hope that you enjoy the freedom that we are seeking. We hope for a better life for you and for us. (Treatment and Rehabilitation Center for Victims of Torture & Dulwich Centre Foundation, 2014, p. 47)

Members of the team at Salam Peace School, Jabaliya, Gaza, with their Kite of Life drawings.

One of the elements of Dr Samah's writings I find most powerful is her insistence that Palestinian mental health workers have a great deal to offer practitioners in different parts of the world:

> Supporting sumud is not only necessary for decolonizing Palestine and liberating its people from oppression, but it also provides an opportunity for Palestinian decolonial mental health to influence mainstream mental health practices. (Jabr, 2025, p. 240)

Palestinian practitioners in the West Bank and Gaza have been influencing narrative practice over the last two decades. Many of their stories of practice are included in *Responding to trauma that is not past: Strengthening stories of survival and resistance* (Treatment and Rehabilitation Center for Victims of Torture & Dulwich Centre Foundation, 2014).

What's more, practitioners from the Palestine Trauma Centre in Gaza, even in the midst of current devastation, are finding ways to honour and elevate children's voices

and agency. The questions they have gathered from Gaza's children are now being circulated widely and used in campaigns (Palestine Trauma Centre, 2024).

The part of Dr Samah's book launch that I found most moving was when she was responding to a member of the audience who is regularly in contact with individuals in Gaza via Instagram, and is struggling with feeling as if their actions of support are not enough. Dr Samah's thoughtful, skilled, caring and strategic response meant a great deal to all who were present:

> Many of us who are not in Gaza see the huge suffering and feel that we can't do enough. And maybe, when we feel our responses are not sufficient, then we get the feeling of emotional burnout. We might feel that nothing we can do is significant. We become resigned and we no longer do anything. This can happen because intentional trauma has the objective of making people feel helpless and it affects people inside Palestine and outside Palestine. I communicate a lot with people in solidarity, and sometimes I see

people overwhelm themselves in their efforts to do something for Palestine. I say, do not deplete yourself and think strategically about what you can do to support. I also say that messages of support are significant. When people look at the Sydney Harbour Bridge [protest march] and see a huge number of people rallying in solidarity, this is very important. This acknowledges Palestinians and their pain, and this has a therapeutic effect that can mitigate the effects of trauma. One of the intended effects of genocide and trauma is to give Palestinians a very dark prospect of the world. It changes the way you see the world, so sending messages of support is significant. When we think of the apathy and neglect of official regimes in the world towards Palestinians, when we think of how the world has allowed all this harm to happen to the people of Gaza for the last two years, we might lose faith in human goodness. The rallies and messages of support and the kind individual communications with some people from outside Gaza and Palestine give Palestinians a message of hope that maintains our common human fabric. I want you to know that this matters a lot to Palestinians. It matters at the psychological level. And now we need to have a separate

conversation about how to make it matter at the political level, because it's political change that needs to occur. But that is a discussion that you should have here. It's for you to organise and strategize and develop effective ways to influence your government.

When I think back to the atmosphere at the book launch and the diversity of people present – Muslim, Jewish, Christian, Hindu, atheist – it seems fitting to close with these words from the book:

> Let's rescue the remains of our humanity from the rubble of Gaza. (Jabr, 2025, p. 28)

Notes

[1] These hopes of researching Sumud remind me of the work of Dr Rita Giacaman (2014, 2018) and her studies of Palestinians' "capacity to endure and resist" (Giacaman, 2014, p. 39).

[2] The Kite of Life was developed in collaboration with the Tamil community in Toronto (see Denborough, 2010).

Dr Samah Jabr was brought to Australia by the Shifa Project.

References

Denborough, D. (2010). *Kite of Life: From intergenerational conflict to intergenerational alliance.* Dulwich Centre Foundation. Available here

Giacaman, R. (2014). Researching health, justice and the capacity to endure. *International Journal of Narrative Therapy and Community Work*, (2), 36–40. Available here

Giacaman, R. (2018). Researching suffering, subjugated knowledge and practices of health: An interview with Rita Giacaman. *International Journal of Narrative Therapy and Community Work*, (4), 70–75. Available here

Jabr, S. (2025). *Radiance in pain and resilience: The global reverberation of Palestinian historical trauma.* Wakefield Press. Available here

Jabr, S., Hinnawi, Z., & Berger, E. (2024). Healing through the skies: Coping with grief through a therapeutic group activity for children in Palestine. *International Journal of Applied Psychoanalytic Studies*, 22(1), e1898 https://doi.org/10.1002/aps.1898

Palestine Trauma Centre. (2024, October 4). Questions from Gaza's Children. *Palestine Trauma Centre UK*. https://www.palestinetraumacentre.uk/news/questions-from-gazas-children

Treatment and Rehabilitation Center for Victims of Torture & Dulwich Centre Foundation. (2014). *Responding to trauma that is not past: Strengthening stories of survival and resistance.* Dulwich Centre Foundation. Available here

White supremacists are in the streets:

What are we to do?

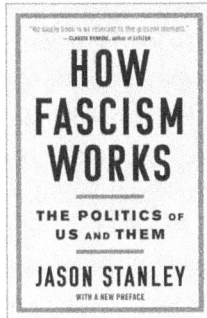

A review of *How fascism works: The politics of us and them* by Jason Stanley in the aftermath of the "March for Australia"

Reviewed by David Denborough

David Denborough (dd) works at Dulwich Centre as a narrative practitioner with individuals, groups and communities who have experienced hardships, and also coordinates the Master of Narrative Therapy and Community Work program at The University of Melbourne.
daviddenborough@dulwichcentre.com.au

ORCID ID: https://orcid.org/0000-0002-3041-3135

Abstract

In the aftermath of the far-right "March for Australia", David Denborough reviews Jason Stanley's (2020) book *How Fascism Works: The politics of us and them*. Penguin. 256pp. ISBN 9780525511854

Key words: fascism; far-right; racism; protest; Jason Stanley; review; narrative therapy; narrative practice

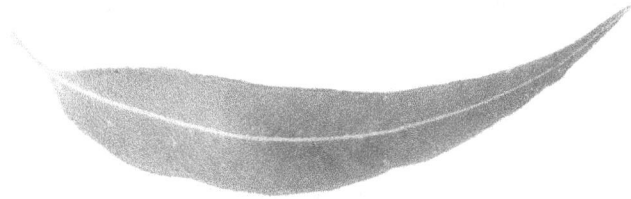

Denborough, D. (2025). White supremacists are in the streets: What are we to do? A review of How fascism works: The politics of us and them by Jason Stanley in the aftermath of the "March for Australia". *International Journal of Narrative Therapy and Community Work*, (2), 95–100. https://doi.org.au/10.4320/JHUP6898

Author pronouns: All pronouns welcome

31 August 2025: Today, across Australia, marches have taken place organised by groups associated with the far right. They marched against immigration and to "stand up to people who hate our country". No foreign flags were allowed but "families were welcome with children". In Melbourne, the most well-known Australian Nazi claimed "his men" had led the march. Some of them, dressed in black, used Australian flag poles to attack a security guard who was protecting a Jewish man. And after the march, the same men viciously bashed Aboriginal women and men at Camp Sovereignty.[1] Here in Adelaide, there was not similar violence, but it was still profoundly disturbing. This was a moment in time when far-right ideology sought to pass itself off as mainstream. We have seen what this can cause in the USA and elsewhere. Now the phenomenon is well and truly here in the city I call home.

White supremacist groups are growing in number in many places, and apparently the leading Australian Nazis are seen as role models to fascists in other countries.[2] My guess is this is in part because of the way these local Nazi groups are successfully reaching out and recruiting people who are struggling, particularly young white men.[3] Nazi organisers empathise with their struggles and provide an explanation for their experiences of hardship. These racist explanations link personal despair to a wider cause: "The reason for the cost-of-living crisis and the housing crisis is immigration". Once personal struggle is linked to these explanations, they provide an avenue for people to join with others. They provide a place for them to train. They create community (a community joined against others). They create forums for action to try to bring about what they see as a preferred future, not only for themselves but for "their people". This provides a sense of "us", a sense of purpose, and a sense of pride.

As I stand watching thousands of Australian flags being held aloft in Rundle Park and then marching down North Terrace, I can sense how people who are participating are feeling empowered by this event. Joyful even. At the same time as I'm holding back tears, it's clear that today is a turning point, and that I need to join with others and take action. There are so many different forms of action that may be required of us in coming months and years, and some of these are eloquently encapsulated by historian Timothy Snyder in his small (2025) book *On Tyranny: Twenty lessons from the twentieth century*. But in this piece, I want to explore possibilities for action for counsellors and community workers more specifically.

Unlike far-right groups, counsellors and community workers do not "recruit" people who are struggling. As the Just Therapy Team of Aotearoa described, we are instead the "receivers of stories of social suffering" (Waldegrave et al., 2003). The Just Therapy Team believes this role is a precious one. In fact, they would say it is "sacred". I associate with secular traditions, but I totally agree that receiving stories of social suffering is an honourable role that also brings considerable responsibilities.

As the far right are marching in our streets, are there additional responsibilities for those of us who are receivers of stories of social suffering? Perhaps there are responsibilities for us to learn from those who are studying far-right groups and those who have studied fascism. Here in Australia, I find the work of Kaz Ross extremely helpful (see Ahmad & Ross, 2025; Kelly, 2025; Ross, 2020). And I have also turned to the book *How Fascism Works: The politics of us and them*. It's by Jason Stanley who is a professor of philosophy and whose Jewish parents lived through the horrors of antisemitism in Western and Eastern Europe. Perhaps we can begin to share resources that we are finding helpful in our respective contexts.

Gender

In his first chapter, Jason Stanley described how a nostalgia for patriarchy is a central organising principle of fascism, and how certain ideals for gender roles define and motivate this political movement. I guess this shouldn't come as a surprise. The current iteration of a "crisis in masculinity", which evokes the need for a return to "traditional masculinity", is in many ways so similar to what was occurring here in the early 1990s. The first *Comment* newssheet published by Dulwich Centre in 1994 was in response to a book from the anti-feminist men's rights movement of the time, *The Myth of Male Power* (Farrell, 1993). In today's march there is a new twist in relation to how patriarchal understandings of gender are fuelling fascism. Some men are wearing t-shirts threatening violence against trans folks. They are, I think, claiming to defend "womanhood". Of course, queer folk are always preferred targets of Nazis.

Racism

While gender is one of the driving organising principles of this march, it's not the main one. This event is clearly mostly about race. There are even signs proclaiming

"White unity at every opportunity". Jason Stanley explained how fascist ideology draws on history in particular ways to create a false vision of a glorious past: "The fascist mythic past exists to aid in *changing the present*" (2020, p. 12). As I watch Australian flags held aloft, it's vividly apparent that racist ideology has plenty of material to work with on this land. Racism justified and enabled genocidal violence against the First Peoples of this land and was the reason why one of the very first acts of the Australian Parliament was the *Immigration Restriction Act 1901* (which came to be known as the White Australia Policy).

Racism has at times been an overwhelming force in this land. Recognition of this makes the achievement of Indigenous resurgence here in Tarntanya (Adelaide) and across the continent all the more remarkable. On the same lands that the march took place, Dr Alitya Rigney described how:

> For the first time since the 19th Century, children in Adelaide are learning Kaurna from birth. Our language, the language of this land, is now well and truly awake.[4]

Acknowledging the pervasive power of colonial racism also backlights the real achievements and joys of multicultural Australia.

This is not the first time this land has had to deal with resurgences of racism. In 1997, racism was surging against Aboriginal people and migrants, and Pauline Hanson (an Australian politician) was its main spokesperson. At that time, as we were seeking ways to talk about the issues and gather together different actions that people were taking, we produced another *Comment* titled "Racism: How can white Australians respond?" (Dulwich Centre, 1997). It feels a bit similar now. Perhaps we can share any initiatives we know of in our respective contexts that are responding to rising racism.[5]

Disparity in wealth and making connections

It also seems relevant to turn our attention to the social conditions that are contributing to the rise of the far right, in particular the growing disparity between rich and poor. Walking through any Australian city these days, it is obvious that the number of folks sleeping rough has increased dramatically, in particular the number of women sleeping on the streets (Pawson et al., 2024). What is much less obvious is that the wealthy are getting so much richer.[6] How can we bring attention to this growing disparity and its consequences in the lives of the people we meet with?

As I mentioned earlier, far-right groups acknowledge suffering – make collective meaning out of it – and use this to recruit people to division and racism. They offer (racist) explanations of despair or marginalisation and funnel it into opposition to others and into hatred. They then enable people to join with others and take action about what they say are the causes of their misery.

As counsellors and people working in social service realms, how are we to respond to social suffering?

- Can we create contexts for those who come to us with stories of suffering to find acknowledgment and explanations that are factual and not based on racism, white supremacy or bigotry?

- Can we create contexts for people to join with others to play some part in redressing and changing the broader factors that are contributing to their suffering?

- Can we create contexts for people to make meaningful contributions to the lives of others – contributions in which they can take pride?

These are some of the principles of collective narrative practice, and I would treasure the chance to collaborate with others who are trying to put them into action at this time of growing inequity in our country.

History

In learning from Jason Stanley about the ways that the far right promulgates divisive mythic versions of the past, this present moment is also challenging me to consider more carefully how I engage with and represent the past. I think of First Nations folks who are honestly grappling with the truth of our histories – including truths within our own family histories – and offering non-Indigenous folks ways forward. I was recently moved by a podcast series entitled *The Descendants* (Allam, 2025; Hannan et al., 2025). Within it, Naaguja Elder Theona Councillor said: "We are not a nation of weaklings. We can handle the truth" (in Allam et al., 2025). I also think of Aunty Barbara Wingard's *Walking History Journey*.[7] Here, narrative practices are used to share double-storied accounts of history in ways that welcome everyone into these stories no matter who you are.

Throughout Aunty Barb's walk, there seems an equal dedication to truth, grace and inclusivity.

As narrative practitioners, when we are working with the stories of people's lives, we are in some ways social historians and cultural workers. We make links across time and across generations. A skill of dignity in the present might be linked to a grandmother's pride, which in turn might be linked to life during World War II or the Depression.

As nostalgic or mythic versions of history are being weaponised, how can we rededicate ourselves to truthful and inclusive versions of history? If this is a question you are interested in, please join me in grappling with it.

Responding to hate

While watching the march from the sidelines, I found myself often thinking of Jewish friends who have already seen synagogues torched in Australia this year, and Muslim friends who have been assaulted in public. I was also thinking of colleagues whose family members have been killed by extremists. Narrative therapist Hina Islam, who lives in Canada, lost members of her family through an anti-Muslim attack by a far-right extremist who was influenced by Australian Nazis. She has subsequently supported a youth coalition in London, Ontario, to transform the site of hate into a site of memory and honouring (see Sathiaseelan, 2025). Alongside her narrative counselling work, Hina is now exploring ways to support young people of all backgrounds to engage in critical thinking (see Heath, 2012, 2024). Hina's work makes me think about what sort of memorials, rituals, songs[8] and critical thinking could be relevant for our counselling and community work here in Australia where hate crimes are also taking place.

My mind flashes also to the work of Chilean feminist activist and narrative therapist Yasna Mancilla Monsalve and her community's responses to lesbian hate crime (Mancilla Monsalve, 2024), and the narrative letter-writing campaign that Belial B'Zarr and Frankie Hanman-Siegersma (2025) initiated in response to anti-trans and anti-drag hate in Melbourne. Narrative practitioners are already responding to hate in skilful ways. While I hope further responses are not needed, I think we need to be prepared. Perhaps we can create some sort of multifaith and multicultural network ready to instantly support colleagues should the need arise. Perhaps we could reach out to those of Camp Sovereignty in the aftermath of the attack there.[9]

Refusing to normalise the once unthinkable

Finally, let me turn to the parts of Jason Stanley's book that I find most moving, when he weaves in the story of his grandmother. He describes how Ilse Stanley ventured into the Sachsenhausen concentration camp, "dressed as a Nazi social worker[10], rescuing from death hundreds of Jews confined there, one by one" (Stanley, 2020, p. 124). Chillingly, during those times in the late 1930s, she struggled to convince her neighbours of the seriousness of the situation. Her grandson implores us to remember this:

> Those who have lived through transitions from democracy to fascism regularly emphasise from personal experience and with great alarm: the tendency of populations to normalise the once unthinkable. (Stanley, 2020, p. 124)

Nazis are now publicly marching on our streets and headlining rallies. This was once unthinkable.

After witnessing the march, we drove across town to see our young Indian friend at the Ganesh Festival. It was delightful to be there. But this year, unlike the previous two festivals I have attended, there were many, many empty seats. Leaders from immigrant communities across Australia encouraged their folks not to go into cities today. The older Indians told my friend they would not allow him to take the bus home tonight. They will drop him home. People are frightened.

This is Australia in 2025.

I write these words to reach out to any of you who might be keen to collaborate. If you are interested in any of the initiatives I have written about here, please reach out to Dulwich Centre Foundation as we seek to explore these realms further.

And I will send this review to Jason Stanley to thank him for his book and for introducing us, via his writing, to his grandmother Ilse Stanley.

Notes

1. Camp Sovereignty was established by Indigenous activists in 2006 in a place that holds significance for First Nations people, having served as a burial site for people from many different First Nations.

2. This was explained by Kaz Ross in a recent interview (Kelly, 2025).

3. I am particularly concerned about reports that far-right groups are specifically targeting, grooming and recruiting young autistic people (see Lovett, 2019; Welch et al., 2023) and simultaneously heartened by the work of Autism Against Fascism (2022).

4. For more about how the Kaurna language has been re-awoken, see Zuckerman (2017). Dr Alitya Rigney's words are from this video.

5. One week after the violence, a free concert was held at Camp Sovereignty with the theme "An attach one one of us is an attack on all of us, so we come together". Scenes and sounds of reclamation can be viewed here: https://www.instagram.com/nitv_au/reel/DOX1q5VAW6x/

6. The wealthiest 200 Australians hold wealth totalling $625 billion, which is the equivalent to nearly a quarter of the total income produced annually in the whole of Australia (Richardson & Stilwell, 2024). The discrepancy between rich and poor has grown substantially in recent times. One in 10 adult Australians are millionaires (due largely to property holdings) (Börger, 2025; Courty, 2025), and yet, 3.3 million people (13.4%) live in poverty (Davidson et al., 2022). Many people are struggling to pay rent and keep up with the cost of living.

7. This walking history journey can be accessed on line at https://vimeopro.com/user5404188/aunty-barb-history-journey An app version can be downloaded from the Apple App Store (search "Aunty Barb Walk") or Google Play (search "Dulwich Centre Walking Tour").

8. If anyone would like to collaborate on songwriting projects as response to the rise of fascism, please get in touch.

9. We have subsequently written and hand-delivered a series of messages to Camp Sovereignty.

10. Reading about Nazi social workers is a confronting reminder of the need for a broader reckoning with social workers' complicity in injustice (see Briskman, 2003; Ioakimidis & Wyllie, 2023; Kunstreich, 2003).

References

Ahmad, R., & Ross, K. (Hosts). (2025, September 3). Anti-immigration rallies and the rise of neo-Nazis [Audio podcast episode]. In *Full Story*. The Guardian. https://www.theguardian.com/australia-news/audio/2025/sep/02/anti-immigration-rallies-rise-of-neo-nazis-full-story-podcast

Allam, L. (Host). (2025, August 4). Decoding a massacre [Audio podcast episode]. In *The Descendants*. The Guardian. https://www.theguardian.com/australia-news/audio/2025/aug/04/the-descendants-episode-1-decoding-a-massacre-full-story-podcast-ntwnfb

Allam, L., Collard, S., & Archibald-Dinge, E. (2025, August 4). These brothers grew up revering their great-uncle Bill. Then the full story came out. *The Guardian*. https://www.theguardian.com/australia-news/2025/aug/04/family-nt-police-constable-bill-mckinnon-history-ntwnfb

Autism Against Fascism. (2022). Autism Against Fascism - Home. Retrieved from https://autismagainstfascism.wordpress.com/

Börger, E. (2025). *Global Wealth Report 2025*. UBS. https://www.ubs.com/us/en/wealth-management/insights/global-wealth-report/_jcr_content/root/contentarea/mainpar/gridcontrol/col_2/actionbutton.0255734011.file/PS9jb250ZW50L2RhbS9hc3NldHMvd20vc3RhdGljL25vaW5kZXgvZ3dyLTIwMjUtZGlnaXRhbC5wZGY=/gwr-2025-digital.pdf

Briskman, L. (2003). Indigenous Australians: Towards postcolonial social Work. In B. Pease, J. Allam, & L. Briskman (Eds.), *Critical social work: An introduction to theories and practices* (pp. 92–106). Allen and Unwin.

B'Zarr, B., & Hanman-Siegersma, F. (2025). Staying alive to prove them wrong: Collaborating with trans people, drag performers and queers in contexts of alt-right violence: An interview with Belial B'Zarr [Video]. *International Journal of Narrative Therapy and Community Work*, (1), https://doi.org/10.4320/NWYL8029

Courty, A. (2025, August 4). Property boom prompts surge in Australian millionaires to global high. *ABC News*. https://www.abc.net.au/news/2025-08-04/property-boom-fuels-surge-in-aussie-millionaires-to-global-high/105589352

Davidson, P., Bradbury, B., & Wong, M. (2022). *Poverty in Australia 2022: A snapshot*. Australian Council of Social Service and UNSW Sydney. https://povertyandinequality.acoss.org.au/wp-content/uploads/2023/03/Poverty-in-Australia-2023_Who-is-affected_screen.pdf

Dulwich Centre. (Ed.). (1994). *Comment*, (1), 1–22. http://dulwichcentre.com.au/wp-content/uploads/2025/09/Comment-gender-politics.pdf

Dulwich Centre. (Ed.). (1997). Racism: How can white Australians respond? [Special issue]. *Comment*, (4), 1–12. https://dulwichcentre.com.au/racism-comment.pdf

Farrell, W. (1993). *The myth of male power*. Simon and Schuster.

Hannan, K. L., & Martignoni, M. (Producers), Allam, L. (Host). (2025). *The Descendants* [Audio podcast]. The Guardian. https://www.theguardian.com/australia-news/series/the-descendants

Heath, M. (2012). On critical thinking. *International Journal of Narrative Therapy and Community Work*, (4), 11–18.

Heath, M. (2024). On critical thinking (M. Heath, Narr.) [Audio recording]. *International Journal of Narrative Therapy and Community Work,* (1). https://doi.org/10.4320/TOGS7956 (Original work published 2012)

Ioakimidis, V., & Wyllie, A. (Eds.). (2023). *Social work's histories of complicity and resistance: A tale of two professions.* Bristol University Press.

Kelly, F. (Host). (2025, August 28). "March for Australia": When grievance and conspiracy collide with Dr Kaz Ross [Radio broadcast and podcast]. *The Radio National Hour.* https://www.abc.net.au/listen/programs/the-radio-national-hour/march-for-australia-when-grievance-conspiracy-collide/105709732

Kunstreich, T. (2003). Social welfare in Nazi Germany: Selection and exclusion. *Journal of Progressive Human Services, 14*(2), 23–52. https://doi.org/10.1300/J059v14n02_02

Lovett, M. (2019). The growing threat of the alt-right: Who are they, how they recruit, and how to prevent further growth. *Security and Society in the Information Age, 2,* 94–111.

Mancilla Monsalve, Y. (2024). We exist and resist as woven patches: Collective narrative practices in an activist context challenging and responding to an anti-lesbian hate crime (M. Shearer, Trans.). *International Journal of Narrative Therapy and Community Work,* (2). 2–19. https://doi.org/10.4320/YTDZ5796

Pawson, H., Parsell, C., Clarke, A., Moore, J., Hartley, C., Aminpour, F., & Eagles, K. (2024). *Australian Homelessness Monitor 2024.* UNSW City Futures Research Centre. https://homelessnessaustralia.org.au/wp-content/uploads/2024/12/AHM_final.pdf

Richardson, D., & Stilwell, F. (2024). *Wealth and inequality in Australia.* The Australia Institute. https://australiainstitute.org.au/wp-content/uploads/2024/08/P1689-Wealth-and-inequality-Updated.pdf

Ross, K. (2020, December 11). Far-right groups have used COVID to expand their footprint in Australia. Here are the ones you need to know about. *The Conversation.* https://theconversation.com/far-right-groups-have-used-covid-to-expand-their-footprint-in-australia-here-are-the-ones-you-need-to-know-about-151203

Sathiaseelan, A. (2025, June 5). London to honour Afzaal family, stand against Islamophobia. *The London Free Press.* https://lfpress.com/news/local-news/london-to-honour-afzaal-family-stand-against-islamophobia

Snyder, T. (2025). *On tyranny: Twenty lessons from the twentieth century.* Penguin Random House.

Stanley, J. (2020). *How fascism works: The politics of us and them.* Penguin.

Waldegrave, C., Tamasese, K., Tuhaka, F., & Campbell, W. (Eds.). (2003). *Just Therapy – a journey: A collection of papers from the Just Therapy Team, New Zealand.* Dulwich Centre Publications.

Welch, C., Senman, L., Loftin, R., Picciolini, C., Robison, J., Westphal, A., Perry, B., Nguyen, J., Jachyra, P., Stevenson, S., Aggarwal, J., Wijekoon, S., Baron-Cohen, S., & Penner, M. (2023). Understanding the Use of the Term "weaponized autism" in an alt-right social media platform. *Journal of Autism and Developmental Disorders, 53,* 4035–4046. https://doi.org/10.1007/s10803-022-05701-0

Zuckerman, G. (2017, March 2). *Professor Ghil'ad Zuckerman in discussion with Dr Alitya Rigney* [Video]. YouTube. https://www.youtube.com/watch?v=Avm86DXjlO4 (Original work published 2011)